The Real Purpose
of
Parenting

D0187677

The Real Purpose

of

Parenting

The Book You Wish Your Parents Read

Dr. Philip Dembo

JACQUIE JORDAN, INC.

THE REAL PURPOSE OF PARENTING

Published by Jacquie Jordan Inc. Publishing

Copyright © 2011 by Dr. Philip Dembo

ISBN: 13 9780981931173

www.tvguestpert.com
www.JacquieJordanIncPublishing.com

Edited by Margie Kaye
Front book cover design by Darice Fisher
Interior book design by Barbara Aronica-Buck
Author photos by Starla Fortunato

DENNIS THE MENACE © 2011 HANK KETCHAM ENTERPRISES.
NORTH AMERICA SYNDICATE

All rights reserved. No part of this publication may be reproduced,
stored in a retrieval system, or transmitted, in any form or by any means,
electronic, mechanical, photocopying, recording, or otherwise, without
prior written permission of the publisher.

First Printing December 2011
Printed in the United States of America
10 9 8 7 6 5 4 3 2 1

The Real Purpose of Parenting:
The Book You Wish Your Parents Read
is dedicated to the memory of one of the greatest kids
who ever lived . . . Jonathan, my stepson,
who passed away when he was only 13-years-old.
Jonathan embodied everything this book is about.
His spirit lives on inside each one of us who knew him
and in each one of the pages of my book.

We miss him dearly.

CONTENTS

ACKNOWLEDGMENTS

There are many people I want to acknowledge and thank for helping me realize this dream of writing my first book, *The Real Purpose of Parenting*. Projects such as this are not accomplished alone.

The profound impact of sharing in the lives of my clients and families is immeasurable. I have learned so much throughout the years and am eternally grateful to each and every one of them for sharing their stories and trusting in me with their concerns.

The Real Purpose of Parenting would never have been written without the guidance and support of my publisher, Jacquie Jordan and Richard Waner of Jacquie Jordan, Inc. Their professionalism and vision have been inspirational for me in this process. I would also like to acknowledge the tremendous support I received from the staff at TVGuestpert.com, including Stephanie Cobian and Jane Shayne.

And with their direction, I have had the privilege to work closely with the talented Margie Kaye, my editor and friend, whose influence is woven throughout this book.

Linda and I are so blessed to be the beneficiaries of the skills and hard work of Nicole Loiterstein, our assistant on all of our projects. We can never thank Nicole enough for all that she does to make our work easier, including the research efforts she put forth on this book.

I need to thank my parents for everything they did to provide me with the life I had growing up. Each in their own way, and together as a couple, they worked so hard to give me and my brother every opportunity this world offers. They did this with all the love and commitment a parent can have for their child. I am eternally grateful to both of them.

To our children, Elizabeth, Jeremy, Rachel, Justin and Adam, I want to thank you for your love, your confidence, and your ever present inspiration as wonderful young men and women. I am so proud of each and every one of you.

And to the love of my life, Linda . . . With you by my side, everything seems possible! I love you more than my words could ever express. You are the true reason I had the courage to write this book.

TO ALL OF YOU . . . Thank you so much for this amazing journey!

My name is Dr. Philip Dembo. I have wanted to write this book for many years, and now that you are holding it in your hands, I cannot express how humble and grateful I feel. I thought it might be helpful to share with you a little bit about who I am and what inspired me to put my thoughts on paper and share them with you. As they say, our children do not come with an instruction manual, so any help I may offer along the way I hope may be useful and welcome. That is my wish, anyway.

I have been a father for 27 years so I understand first hand what an important and often daunting role being a parent can be. I am the dad of two grown kids (Are they ever really?) . . . Elizabeth, who is 27 and Justin, who is 21. I am also a proud and dedicated stepfather of three children; Rachel, 23, Adam, 21 and Jonathan, in blessed memory, who would now be 17. I also recently took on another role, as a father-in-law to Jeremy, 27, Elizabeth's husband.

I am married to the most amazing woman I have ever known, Linda. She is my perfect partner. I do not think that I had ever experienced the true feeling and meaning of love until I looked into her beautiful blue eyes on that fateful Friday in August, 2006. (I say fateful because the life experiences that brought us together are the makings of another book, maybe even a movie, but I must reserve those for a later date.) Linda and I have been together and connected ever since we first spoke, in what many remark is a fairy tale courtship unlike any other they have witnessed. It seems so natural for us both however, we never for a moment take it for granted. We just relish in our togetherness each and every day.

I am Director of Life Strategies, a coaching and consulting firm. In my 30- year professional career as a therapist and life coach, I have spent literally thousands of hours with couples, families, parents and kids, assisting them with the strategies necessary to have successful experiences. These experiences only reinforce for me, my need to write this book to you, not as a therapist, not as a life coach, but . . . from one parent to another.

My frame of reference growing up presented itself at an early age as I was born with Scoliosis (curvature of the spine) and was destined for a life punctuated by physical pain. For the first fifteen years of my life, my parents made straightening my spine their mission and MY identity. With all loving intentions, I was taken from doctor to doctor, procedure to procedure, yielding no real success. Everything available medically today for the treatment of Scoliosis, was either not suitable or too risky for me then.

From age seven to twelve, my torso was wrapped into a plaster body cast. I'm not sure if it helped my spine, but it clearly did little for my social life and self-esteem. You see, this was my first realization that in families, parents can be driven more by what something "looks like" than by "what it is." My voice didn't seem to matter to them. My feelings were never questioned; my physical pain was never discussed, BUT looking like everyone else was always the goal; FOR THEM! The more they pursued their goal, the less I felt I looked normal at all. My parents were GREAT people, don't get me wrong, and I know that they were not trying to be intentionally cruel. They just believed what many believe in our society; if a child looks or acts like everyone else, they will feel "normal." For them, normal WAS self-esteem.

Throughout my personal and professional journey, I have been motivated by the internal struggle I feel that we in society, continue to "miss the boat" on what we must create in order to maximize the potential in every person. I am struck by this belief system we (still) embrace; the notion that "different" is judged negatively. Somehow we are made to feel that we must be the same in order to be accepted. This misconception controls our culture, directs our values and morals and subsequently, guides the parenting of our children. How is it that the judgment has woven itself into our norms, our culture? We seem to know so much about so many things, yet we resist the change necessary in our attitude to allow ourselves to evolve as individuals. My friends, parents ARE those assigned with the responsibility to protect the "individual" in each child.

There is much to do and it won't be easy to make the necessary changes to honor growth of the individual when we have judged and controlled for so very long. We must create a collective conscience in the culture by developing the conscience of each individual, one child at a time.

We must change the way we have been parenting. If we learn to develop that conscience, that self regulatory process in each individual, we will raise kids to live out there in the world as individuals . . . fully developed and with a healthy sense of self.

WELCOME to *The Real Purpose of Parenting*. Let's get busy.

DISCLAIMER

Throughout my 30-year career as a therapist and a life coach, I have had the pleasure of sharing in the lives and stories of literally thousands of families.

The names and details of some of my encounters have been altered to respect the privacy and integrity of the relationships I have developed with these families over the years.

All of the stories depicted in this book could represent any number of actual families, and no one family is being singled out. Please try to experience the message in the stories rather than merely searching through its details for some familiarity.

It is my hope that you can relate to and gather insights from all of the material included, and realize that in reality, we are all depicted here, in one way or another.

Thank you.

"IT WASN'T MY FAULT, MOM! MY CONSCIENCE
TALKED ME INTO IT!"

CHAPTER ONE

From One Parent to Another

Any parent who frequents a library or most any book store will certainly find rows and rows of books on parenting. And so you may wonder, what would possess someone to tackle the subject again and write yet *another* parenting book, thinking that in any way possible it would have something different to say or add to the dialogue on this ever frustrating and complex topic of being a parent in today's world?

I came to the conclusion that although there are numerous wonderful books on parenting, as with most important topics and issues, the more perspectives we gather the better. So, I encourage you to search through these books and find the ideas that resonate with you most. I ask only that you read THIS book . . . FIRST!

I am a parent just like most of you. I am someone else's child just like all of you. I have my observations, experiences and opinions as each of you do. My goal is to share with you my conclusions and suggestions based on being a son, being a father and having the opportunity, professionally for 30 years to share intimately in the lives of thousands of families just like yours and mine.

As I sit here today writing this book I recognize that I made many mistakes as a son, and many more as a parent. So I am writing this for me as much as I am writing this for you.

I work hard everyday of my life to be a good parent and make the necessary changes in order not to make those mistakes anymore. Once you are a child, you seem to always be a child. Once you are a parent, you are always going to be a parent. The big question is . . . what kind of parent are you going to be and are you willing to change what's necessary to be effective?

This book is about all of us and the culture we live in. It is not about divorced families or kids with ADD, or drug addiction, or the latest trends in potty training per se. Those are topics you'll find in the other specialty books. This is a book about the thread that runs through all of the issues, all diagnoses, all children, all parents and all families. This is about raising a conscience as you raise a child.

Let me tell you a story . . . About 10 years ago I met 17-year-old Brian Smith and his parents in my office. They came to me after years of struggle between the three of them, mainly about Brian's lack of effort in school.

The Smiths are a strong Catholic family, financially successful and overall very pleasant people. Brian was in his spring semester, senior year at his second private, all boys Catholic High School. He was asked to leave the first school he attended after his sophomore year because of poor grades and disrespectful behavior.

Brian was failing two classes at his current school and his parents were fearful he was not going to graduate "on time." They brought him to me to coach him into becoming a "student" capable of pulling his grades up enough so that he could graduate with his class and go off to college . . . "like everyone else."

The difficulty here was that the "truth" was inconsistent with the "picture" the parents had for their son. This wasn't about whether Brian was capable enough to do well. That discussion, frankly, had long passed. The truth in front of us was that Brian had no intention of being a student. Therefore, he was unwilling to put forth the effort to meet the goals of his parents. Unfortunately for everyone, no one was willing to have *that* conversation.

With four weeks left in the semester, five weeks to commencement, the parents had to do something. So, they brokered a deal with the private high school, which, by the way, you cannot broker with the public schools in our community, to allow Brian to "walk" with his class in the graduation ceremony with an empty diploma sleeve. He would then attend summer school after graduation and complete the classes necessary to fill the sleeve with a "real" diploma.

Why? Because the Smiths were mortified about Brian's truth and couldn't face his grandparents or the community and tell them the truth that Brian chose not to perform as a student and did not complete his necessary requirements.

So, the ILLUSION of success was much more important to them than the TRUTH of Brian. Brian was not a student.

Graduation came as did the elaborate graduation party the Smiths orchestrated for Brian. His grandparents, extended family and friends all attended the festivities and each and every one of them was so proud of his accomplishments.

The main question of the day was . . . "So what college have you decided on?"

What *college* have you decided on? (Are you kidding me? . . . Sorry!)

Brian and his parents put brave confident smiles on their faces and without hesitation, gave an answer pleasing to all in attendance. You see, the Smiths brokered another deal. They had to, because once you replace a truth with an illusion, you must keep it going in order to present the picture you want the world to see. If Brian was indeed graduating with everyone, he was certainly going off to college with everyone. Brian's parents found a college with low requirements that were willing to admit him on probation. Good for Brian, good for the Smiths.

Summer came and went with much struggle and emotion. The Smiths could not understand how Brian didn't see the importance of his summer school class performance. Brian went off to school kicking and screaming. Mrs. Smith actually had to write several of his papers for him, but by God, they accomplished their goal and Brian (and his mother) passed both classes.

His parents received his diploma in the mail, slid the document into its vacant sleeve, and all of a sudden, the illusion became the truth; same old dynamics, same old pattern.

Move-in day was a wonderful milestone for Brian and the Smiths. Their little boy was going off to college, creating stories they could share with their contemporaries. For Brian, he was finally getting away from the scrutiny, the nagging, the fighting, the rules. He was finally free.

Everybody says . . . " That's just normal. Every kid feels that way and every parent deserves that joy of seeing their child off to their next step in life."

Big sigh . . . Who is "everybody" anyway? Who comes up with these norms that we must attach our truth to, in order to create these pictures? (Sorry, don't get me started on this now . . . more later!)

The semester went on peacefully and without incident. Mrs. Smith would call Brian everyday to make sure Brian was getting up and going to his class, doing his homework and making friends, just like everyone else! Brian, of course, reassured her that he was doing well, working hard and making great friends.

Brian was asked to leave the university by November of his first semester. Remember, he was accepted on probation, so there was no room for "brokering" here. He needed to maintain a 2.0 grade point average throughout the semester to remain in school.

In my office as voices were emotionally charged, the Smiths had come to realize that they could no longer hide from the truth . . . Brian was not a student! That statement meant the unthinkable to them; that Brian was a failure and would/could never amount to anything remotely successful.

By the way, there was never a readiness on the part of the Smiths to discuss the dishonesty they promoted, or the self-esteem of their child who could never seem to please them. There was never room for the conversation of what might have happened if they had a different attitude, took a different approach, listened to the struggle behind their son's resistance.

Upon my recommendation, by the way, the first bit of advice that the

Smiths actually followed, Brian moved out on his own and into an apartment with a roommate. He was now *finally* responsible for himself. He needed to find a job, work full time, pay his bills and find his own path. The Smiths saw this as a tragic failure and were ashamed at this course of action. As a result, they pulled away from their son for a very long while.

Brian however thought he was on Easy Street. Finally, no school, plenty of freedom and his parents off of his back!

I didn't hear from any of the Smiths for about 18 months until one day, as I was sitting in my inner-office, an odor was permeating my waiting room. I walked out into the outer area of my office suite, only to find Brian Smith sitting there in tears. The odor, by the way, was emanating from him. I knew that familiar smell. Anyone who ever washed dishes in a restaurant, or worked around deep fryers in a greasy spoon would know that smell all too well. I had the good fortune of exuding those odors myself while working throughout high school and college.

Brian had been working two jobs to make ends meet, but his ends were never truly meeting. He asked me if I remembered him. How could I forget? I remember all the wonderful kids and families I have had the good fortune to meet. I had a free hour so I invited him inside for some privacy.

Brian's first words out of his mouth were . . . "I get it now. I don't want to work this way the rest of my life. I have no freedom and I have no money. Will you help me?"

We spent several visits exploring the feelings that led him to his choices. We created from those feelings a plan that reflected his goals. He wanted to stay in the food industry, because he knew he wouldn't do what was necessary to finish school; because Brian now could speak to his own truth. Brian was not a student.

We both agreed that he still required some form of training if he was to accomplish his goal and move up the food chain; pun *intended!* With a touch of good strategy, (if I may say so myself,) some re-educating his parents to who their son was, an honest letter and a very good interview,

Brian was admitted to The New England Culinary Institute.

Today, Brian Smith is the assistant head chef at a very fancy, five-star hotel. He earns a great salary, has great benefits and most importantly, a great attitude.

So, what were the Smiths so afraid of? Who defined for them this standard for their son? How is it that somehow all the years of judgment, conflict, power struggles, yelling, shame, hiding, lying, and illusion were worth continuing when they NEVER produced the results they were looking for? What was wrong with the truth of who Brian was? Failure was so large for them it was to be avoided at all costs! Failure, like success is an experience to be learned from and embraced. Was Brian's outcome more important than the process of his development and the quality of the time they spent with him? This is all about the Smiths JUDGMENT versus Brian's TRUTH!

We will talk about "judgment" later on in this book, but it's important here to note that when we talk about judgment, we are not talking about what a parent believes is right for their child. We are talking about parents not accepting what is real, specific and truthful about their child, regardless of what they may believe is the right script.

Ultimately and eventually, the truth of our child, and **their** view of **their** experience will have to be attended to, but at what cost? If we don't find a way to empower our child to have their own experience while holding them to a set of standards we believe in, we will raise them with a distorted view of themselves. That's the real trick, isn't it? Recognizing the fine line between **our** agenda as the parent and **their** experience as a separate identity based on their view of the world as they grow up in ours! We, as parents can set the culture of expectations as we see them, but we cannot control how our children experience that world.

We are all the Smiths in one way or another. We all have stories where the picture of what we were hoping for was so much more important to us than what we were actually dealing with in front of us. Maybe our judgments are not as profound and our control and power are not as impactful as what Brian experienced, but are all unhealthy in the raising of our children, nonetheless.

Think of the level of judgment we must have and the comparative analysis required in order to fit our children into a picture when they actually don't fit. Think what we must be doing to the self-esteem of our children when we give them the message that who they are is only good enough when it coincides with the picture we have created for them. They must fit! Think about what this must mean to the development of our child's **"psyche" . . . the place where one's ethics, morals, character and personality develop together to create one's identity, one's integrity.**

We must change our own attitude as parents and learn a different way.

The parenting models of the past 50 years, post World War II have all addressed the self-esteem and ways for parents to attend to their child's development. But they have all fallen short in helping us understand what we really must do in order to help children develop their psyche fully; it's harder today than ever.

The world our children are growing up in is faster, colder, and more intense than ever before. We do not have a collective self-esteem in this culture. We have groups of people, vigilantly trying to look like one another. We have celebrity golfers, governors, actors and presidents who make decisions that hurt many other people but who are heralded for their confessions and remorse.

Our children are growing up in a world where the "picture is definitely greater than the truth." It's everywhere; on the internet, television, and every social media outlet. Our children are surrounded with these stories and our collective tolerance of the lack of integrity.

We seem to have generation after generation of highly competent individuals growing up, knowing how to do many wonderful things I could never have imagined when I was a child. Yet, we see more and more of these young adults unable to self-regulate. We see more and more of these young adults who clearly know right from wrong, but don't really care. We see these young people doing whatever it is they wish to do for their own amusement, regardless of who it hurts.

Remember the young Rutgers University student who committed suicide because a group of his "friends" played a practical joke and videotaped him kissing another young man in the privacy of his room, and put it out onto the internet? Their amusement was more important at that moment than his feelings. His truth was overruled by their agenda. Is there a correlation between the Smiths' story and these young people I mention? You bet there is!

The truth of one's experience, without someone else's judgment, is critical to the development of the individual's psyche, their conscience and their ability to self-regulate out in the world. Brian Smith found his way to what he wanted to do in life. He found what his standard was for himself, by the true experience he felt while trying to make it on his own. He has well meaning and loving parents that, under a different model, with a different attitude, could have been along his side, guiding him, coaching him and loving him as he practiced his own view of the world while growing up in theirs. Instead, they parented as they were taught to parent, and tried to take full responsibility and control for orchestrating Brian's experience and his outcome. Brian fought back to get through. The struggle was large, the development of his self was muted, the bond between them was entrenched in trauma, and the underdevelopment of his identity was evident.

Parents have the responsibility to nurture the truth in their children without their own judgment becoming the agenda, so that their child can fully develop a clear sense of themselves, a clear sense of their conscience, without having to spend much of their efforts finding a way around their parents' reaction.

Being a parent is a daunting and overwhelming responsibility. Although we are doing so many things right today as parents, and we know so much more about parenting than our parents did, we are still doing it within an attitude and in a culture that is a step off of where it needs to be.

We must get our parenting in sync with our child's true development. For you new parents, I ask you to consider adopting this model of thinking and learn the necessary strategies and steps to protect the development of your child.

For those of you who have already started parenting, we must undo what we have already done and embrace a new attitude. And for those who already parent, protecting your child's experience while guiding, coaching and loving them through it . . . call me!

CHAPTER TWO

Raising a Conscience
While Raising a Child

I need to apologize to you ahead of time! This is a chapter in the book that we will need to get through together, with patience and purpose.

When looking to change any type of attitude or thinking, we must have a new framework from which to operate. In order to take on that task, we must first visit history, theory, and create new definitions for the language of our new thinking.

After World War II, society began to settle back down, heal, and prosper. Babies were being born in record numbers. Urban sprawl was everywhere and communities were being established to accommodate the large number of new families. The generation we now call "The Baby Boomers" were being born and their parents were setting out to live the "dream." (I was born in 1957 at the tail end of the Baby Boom. My parents took my brother and me and moved to our new home in the North Shore suburbs of Chicago.)

A popular new invention called the television became a permanent fixture in every house. With that addition came information, education and possible alternatives to how we had currently been doing things . . . including parenting.

The family as we knew it began to evolve. We saw an evolution and progression in the thinking of what constitutes effective parenting. As society shifted, our view of the development of the child shifted. As we adjusted to this new perception, parents needed new thinking and the necessary new skills to embrace and attend to the day-to-day issues that would come up with their children.

Over the next 60 years, families were inundated with new theories, models, and ideas. So much so, that we now question every move and decision we make when it comes to all of the complex issues related to raising children.

In the 1950's, Dr. Benjamin Spock was "the man." His advice focused on a child's self-esteem, rather than just their performance, outcome and success. This was groundbreaking material that now resonated throughout the land.

This new thinking led to the beginning of a fundamental new concept in parenting: the self-esteem and the notion that preventing failure and negative experiences was an important way to keep the self-esteem of our children whole. For Dr. Spock, children needed to feel success in order to feel good about themselves, rather than processing the failure as an experience that inevitably occurs in one's life. He connected self-esteem to successful moments. Raise your child to feel good about themselves through success, praise and affirmation was his advice. It really was groundbreaking! The self-esteem is critical to raising healthy children.

Just a side note here . . . When I first learned about Dr. Spock, I envisioned him to look like Leonard Nimoy with pointy ears and a monotone voice, only to realize later on that Dr. Spock was *not* Mr. Spock from the television show, Star Trek! (I told you television became a powerful fixture in every home back then!)

Dr. Spock's beliefs and advice were important and much of what he taught is still relevant today. However, the self-esteem in children cannot be whole without a clear understanding that every experience is an experience to fully embrace.

It turns out that JUDGING FAILURE AS A NEGATIVE and success as the only POSITIVE has been FATAL to the full development of a child's identity and conscience. I am sure that Dr. Spock could not have predicted the intense competitive world we have morphed into. Had he done so, he may have taken his theory a bit further, understanding the possible complications of attaching self-esteem to performance, in a world where success is pursued at the risk of integrity.

Ultimately, his philosophy had an inverse effect on what he set out to teach.

Avoidance of truthful moments, that are judged to be failure, for the protection of a child's self-esteem, has proven to be central to the underdevelopment of a child's psyche.

It turns out that this paradigm creates an incomplete developmental process in the support and enhancement to one's conscience. Why? Because if an experience is judged as failure (negative) and considered non-permissible, avoidance of that failure becomes more the goal of the experience than what you actually may feel or learn from that moment.

Let me say that again . . . if an experience is judged as failure (negative) and considered non-permissible, avoidance of failure becomes more the goal of the experience than what you may actually feel or learn from that moment. Avoidance of failure becomes more important than even the process of success! Crazy, right? But true!

Success "at all cost" brings with it the potential for dishonesty, for short cuts, for hiding the truth, and for numbing oneself to the feelings of what one is experiencing.

The picture of success will override the truth of the authentic experience. We justify that by believing that the truth of failure will be too devastating to the self-esteem of the child. But, in reality, truth of any kind is fundamental to the self-esteem of the child! It's the JUDGMENT of that truth that puts the self-esteem at risk. And it's the voice of the parent who brings the judgment that gets in the way of the child feeling their full experience.

Experiencing the full experience without interference by anyone else's judgment allows for one's own internal voice, one's psyche to process the experience. This creates a healthy confident, truthful self.

As I said before, Dr. Spock could not have predicted that society would have morphed into what it is today. The notion that promoting successful experiences to promote a good self-esteem may have evolved into a cultural paradigm where success is the only goal and failure is to be judged was unpredictable. Now parents feel the overwhelming responsibility of making sure their child is successful in order to preserve their child's self-esteem (and probably theirs as well!)

Dr. Spock's assertion has been centrally woven into our collective belief system over the past 60 years. Our culture relies on it to make sense of it and for each individual to make sense of themselves. It is fundamental in all the parenting models that have followed.

It will be quite the task to alter these attitudes and beliefs, but we must take it on and we must make the change. If we do not, we will find more and more generations growing up incomplete and unable to cope honestly with the experiences in their lives.

In the1960's and 1970's, theories like Dr. Thomas Gordan's *"Parent Effectiveness Training,"* (PET) focused on the communication patterns between parent and child and the skills necessary for effective communication. This theory suggests that if you were effective in your communication with your child in a "democratic" dynamic, you will be able to empower their ability to talk to you and they will therefore feel good about themselves.

Effective communication in families is necessary no matter what the philosophical approach, and I encourage you to embrace skills that work for you.

In the 1970's and 1980's the notion of "natural and logical consequences" were presented to parents through new models like *"Systematic Training for Effective Parenting,"* (STEP) by Dinkmeyer and McKay. This was another huge step forward in our understanding of the child's experience as it relates to our parenting and intervention.

Consequences, both natural and logical are also important to understand in the parenting of children. In today's parenting, consequences, understandably, have become an example of "failure!"

And you now know what I feel that judgment does to kids, don't you?

We will address this concept and where it fits in a child's experience later on in the book.

From the 1990's until today, we have theories that are well developed in the empowerment of children and more specifically about the role of a parent. Theories such as *"Love and Logic,"* by Dr. Foster Kline and Jim Faye, speak to the "choices a child makes and parents' encouragement of the child to think for themselves. Dr. Kline is best known for his work with children with "attachment issues" and the damage these kids have had to their character development. These are very important concepts to be learned. Dr. Kline, too has pushed us forward as a collective body of parents trying to stay in step with the rate in which our society is influencing our child's growth.

All of these theories and models of parenting are relevant today and each have components that you will find helpful and effective. I encourage you to explore them all. HOWEVER . . . I still believe that they all fall short in addressing this fatal flaw in our attitude toward healthy parenting. Parents must operate differently!

Judgment and comparative analysis, success and failure as a standard for self-esteem are not only unmotivating and diminishing to the child, they also do not allow the self to develop completely.

Most parents will tell you it feels almost impossible to keep up with the ever changing cultural issues that they face raising children today. PARENTING IS OVERWHELMING! The character flaws out there in our society today that children are exposed to are pervasive and very disturbing.

Let's revisit our good friend, Brian Smith from Chapter One for a short minute . . .

Do you remember when Brian reappeared back in my waiting room in tears, smelling like the backroom of a greasy spoon? I made mention then that Brian and I had a few visits and reflected on his feelings that led to his resistance to being a student and the ongoing power struggle with his parents. Brian Smith had low self-esteem, of course. He was afraid of growing up. He was afraid of performing. He was afraid of trying. Brian told me stories about the reactions his parents had to his ideas from as early as three years of age. If they agreed with him they celebrated loudly, and if they disagreed, they condemned loudly as well. He told me of times when he was scolded for missing a basket in a ballgame when he was 5-years-old. He told me of times he was praised so intensely for getting a good grade, you would have imagined that he saved someone's life. It was amazing the details he remembered from these everyday interactions. These were not major incidents in life, but they had become so to Brian. And he also told me of the violent reactions he had toward his parents' positive and negative judgments (reactions!)

Let's be honest for a second. Brian's example may be a bit extreme, but we have all either experienced our parents reacting that way, or we have reacted that way to our own children.

Brian's conclusion was poignant. He had come to realize while experiencing life on his own, that he made his parents' reactions his excuse not to try. It was easier to blame them, and to feel something about their reaction, rather than ever allowing himself to feel his feelings about his own choices and experiences.

Let's talk about how conscience development works . . . Remember when your child was born? What an amazing moment to experience . . . for the child! You see, when a child is born, they are UNIVERSAL. The whole human condition is an experience, and an experience is the whole human condition.

The baby's conscience, personality, values system, moral structure, are all one entity; one experience. So, when a baby is held, they feel something. When they aren't held, they feel something as well. When they want to be held they cry, and when we pick them up, they coo. Their feelings, their thoughts, their needs and their wants are all experienced fully and without connection to anyone else. When that same baby is hungry, they give us the same response to their hunger as they do to their need to be held, or have their diaper changed for that matter.

self-esteem, self-worth, loving one's self, success and failure are concepts that do not exist in the psyche of a baby. They don't have to exist as separate consciousness because babies are fully in their moment. They are fully experiential and complete. It is all one experience.

Parents begin the process of figuring out what the baby is feeling, thus attending to the needs of the feelings expressed. (So, why do we stop focusing on the child's feelings of their experience as they begin to communicate with language? I don't get it!) What changes that approach as the baby grows? (More on that soon.)

When a child first begins to experience the COMPARATIVE nature of performance, that is when they first experience the notion that their feelings are to be experienced separately.

The first moment when behavior is no longer just an experience but a PERFORMANCE to be evaluated and judged, reacted to by someone else's view, is when a child begins to see themselves in comparison to others. The child looks to the parents' reaction to make sense of themselves. They no longer feel the experience completely because they are looking outside their experience to determine whether someone else feels pleased with them.

Let's face it; performance is an inevitable plight for all human beings in the world as it is. I certainly am NOT suggesting that we try to find a way to create a culture in which the universal experience would be preserved throughout a lifetime. (I may be good, but no one is *that* good!) I am certainly NOT suggesting that we eliminate performance in any way. However, I do believe that there is another way to approach it while protecting the process of the conscience.

I AM suggesting that a baby's universal experience gives us insight into how intact the psyche is when a baby first arrives and how inconsistent and conflict ridden our daily culture is with the natural expression of the human condition. Let's take a breath here for a second before we move on . . .

Here's a little story that illustrates my point . . . I began playing tennis in my late 40's and joined a class that met on Thursday nights. Our class had participants from 21 to 65 years of age. A group of us became very close friends and would go out after class for a bite to eat and would talk well into the night. After a while, we continued our friendship outside of class and met regularly for social events. One young couple in the group became parents to a beautiful little boy, Sam. I was there at the hospital, a day after the delivery to visit, so I met Sam right at birth, if you will.

Sam, like all babies, was absolutely universal. He was happy to be here, happy to be fed, happy to be held, and let it be known when he wasn't and needed something.

I got busy with work, and family and tennis, and Sam and his parents got busy getting to know one another. I went to visit Sam and his parents about four months later and of course, Sam had grown considerably. Here is what I witnessed . . .

After the oohs and ahhs about Sam subsided, Sam was laid down on a blanket so his parents could attend to their guests and socialize freely. Sam was content on his blanket, while always keeping an eye on one of his parents. When they would begin to get wrapped up in a conversation, he would begin to scream and cry so that they would refocus their attention back to him. Without hesitation, his parents would excuse themselves and refocus on Sam until he settled back down.

Sam put his parents through this dance 14 times (I counted!) and with each episode, everyone kept trying to figure out what Sam needed. I just kept quiet. (It's difficult doing what I do for a living and being out socially because everyone looks to me for answers!)

Sam knew what reactions to create in his parents. And in an effort to attend to him (actually keep him quiet) and have a nice evening with their friends, they were willing to dance the dance.

Here's what else I observed . . . Sam's parents were embarrassed by Sam's inability to lay still and play quietly. They wanted so badly for their son to perform well in front of others and make a good showing. What other people thought of Sam mattered (to them) and how he behaved was judged as success or failure. Sam was a four month old beautiful boy and he was already being comparatively analyzed by what was supposed to be and what was actually happening! Just being Sam was already not good enough. He was expected to perform . . . .and he did . . . but *his* way. The truth was that you could see that Sam was in reaction to his parents and the more they tried to get him to behave a certain way, the more he danced his dance . . . and he was only four months old!

Break's over . . . let's forge ahead . . .

Every experience is filtered through ones PSYCHE. **The psyche is the processing center that blends our values, morals, intellect, personality and spirit into our identity.** From that blending comes a process that allows us to view the world through our own interpretation. **This is our CONSCIENCE!**

This becomes each individual's "TRUE PERSONAL WORLD VIEW;" how one sees the world and how one chooses to operate in the world they see. It isn't JUST our understanding of "right and wrong," but our choice of how we represent ourselves and experience the decisions of right and wrong. This, by the way, is where we have gotten ourselves in trouble as a collective society.

Teaching kids right from wrong was thought to be enough in our world. We never imagined or questioned whether children would detach from their feelings of the moment. We just assumed that if they knew the difference between right from wrong, they would act accordingly.

Parents must understand what I am suggesting here. There must be a way to teach our values, our preferences, our culture, to our child while protecting the "processing center;" their psyche and its development. We must believe in the protection of that "universal state" as much as possible, in a world where performance and competition, comparison and judgment are realities in their lives. Both must find a way to coexist, otherwise, the processing center will alter itself to operate in reaction to external influences.

Think about this . . . if a child has a fully developed self, without interference by others' judgment, in their true personal world view, they will be comfortable making choices based on their own experience. The implication of this becomes dramatic when a child's peer relationships become more influential than their parents are to them. The pressure of peers' expectations become less of a struggle for a healthy self-esteem. Children will not be as conflicted in their choices based on what their friends think because their psyche, their conscience has developed to see the world comfortably through their own experience and not someone else's.

They will be less inclined to be influenced by what they see on television or the Internet. The stories of their favorite celebrity or political leader and the less than integral choices they just made and behaviors they are caught up in will be news worthy but *not* a model for their own choice. Children will grow to be comfortable in "their own skin" when they are NOT influenced by the reaction and stories of others.

Today, more than ever, children (and parents) identify themselves based on what they think in reaction to what others think. There seems to be a disconnect from the feelings of their own experience in exchange for the view of someone else. This breeds fear and anxiety, not just to perform but to perform a certain way to elicit a certain response. (Remember baby Sam!)

Human beings are born with the "complete experience" intact. A complete experience is when our feelings and thoughts of our experience in the moment are in sync with our feelings and thoughts about self-worth and identity. We as a culture have built a life experience that forces us away from that complete moment. Yet, we really do need that process as we navigate through the performance of life in order to keep the psyche and the conscience functioning, untainted by the process of others.

So the experience that starts with a child must be experienced by the child and end with the child with little or no interference from the experience of another person. The experience must be as universal as we can get it, given the world we live in.

EVERY MOMENT'S EXPERIENCE BEGINS WITH A FEELING!

Yes it's true! The universal experience is still alive in all of us. It's human. We experience a feeling in every moment first, before a thought or a choice.

The challenge is to identify the feeling that defines the moment for us and wrap our thoughts around that feeling uninterrupted by the agenda of others. Here is the true process of our experience . . .

FEELING . . . THOUGHT . . . DECISION . . . ACTION.

We feel the moment, create a thought from those feelings and make a decision to take action based on our original feeling. When we create a thought from the feeling of the moment, all that we have learned and experienced that is relevant to the moment results in that thought. From that we make our decision and take action.

It all happens in a split second and it happens continually throughout our daily experience. Parents must trust this process as being healthy. Children will make choices consistent with their experience, based on the feeling of the experience and the knowledge they have gained from previous experiences. Parents may be uncomfortable with the potential decision the child will make, but they must resist "taking over" the moment with their own agenda.

A feeling is the internal experience that creates emotion. Emotion is the feeling's expression of itself. A thought is the cognition we wrap around the feeling and emotion. It is the logical construct around the feeling that helps us make sense of our experience, honoring the feeling and incorporating one's frame of reference. From that thought, we can make decisions and take action.

The intention of the feeling, the reason "why" we are feeling what we are feeling in the moment creates our identity. It is our truth!

In society today, we do not communicate between feeling and thought, where the truth of the experience and identity lie. We are taught to communicate between thought and decision where interpretation, manipulation and defensiveness may prove necessary.

If the agenda of someone else interferes with the experience we are having, we detach ourselves from the feeling of the experience and the thoughts we are having about those feelings. Our thoughts abandon the original feeling and attach themselves to DEFENDING against the judgment. We redirect to the feelings we have about the judgment in front of us. We separate ourselves from the experience and spend our consciousness questioning the validity of our own feelings and the value of our identity as it compares to the view of "everyone else." self-esteem gets challenged. Now the goal of finding one's self in the standards of someone else's picture replaces the confidence of experiencing one's own feelings in one's own moment.

This produces insecurity, anxiety and fear that we are not "good enough" unless we compare favorably with the world around us set forth by the agenda (the picture) parents have for our identity.

I must go on record here as saying to you that I am not implying that parents should sit back and have no input into their child's life. I am saying that what that input looks like and where that intervention punctuates in the process of experience is VITAL to protecting identity development and the ability of a child to self-regulate into adulthood.

Let me introduce you to Molly Cook . . . I met Molly when she moved back to town. She was 28-years-old upon her return. I met her family while she was living elsewhere in pursuit of her career. The Cooks are prominent people in our community. Their level of prominence is so great that if you mentioned the family name, most everyone in town would know exactly who you are referring to.

Along with that stature for Mr. and Mrs. Cook came a sense of power, protocol and pedigree. There was a clear expectation that all of their children follow their agenda in terms of career, life partners, zip code to call home and churches to belong to.

Molly followed a career path unacceptable to her parents. The conflict was constant and volatile. The Cooks saw no room for compromise here and relentlessly pursued Molly until Molly relented.

Molly at 28, moved back to her parents' home, without having a job or a career path. She felt defeated at the hands of her parents' judgment. Depression, low self-esteem and hopelessness followed.

Molly's feelings of her own experience were long replaced with thoughts dedicated to the defense of herself with her parents. Exhausting long talks and heated debate continued to define their relationship.

Molly operated in her process between "thought" and "decision" because that was where she could deal with her parents' judgment of her natural choices. The detachment from her feelings of her experience was necessary to harden her from their judgment. She felt too vulnerable, feeling her feelings while defending her position. Molly could not see herself at all without seeing her parents first.

For her, the conflict inside was huge. It really wasn't a conflict about her parents anymore. For Molly, it was the conflict that she couldn't feel her own truth. She didn't know if it was her own experience, her parents' agenda, or simply a rebellious reaction to their picture.

Mr. and Mrs. Cook didn't really see Molly working much longer anyway. It was time to find the "right" man and get married. The problem here was that every suitor Molly found interesting and appealing, either didn't have the pedigree necessary or the right level of income to please her parents.

Molly kept losing those fights as well. She walked away from several men she really liked because they would never be accepted by her parents. She finally agreed to date Michael. Michael met the criteria and Mr. and Mrs. Cook quickly fell in love with him for Molly.

Within a year, Molly was engaged, deposits were put down for the wedding, and invitations were printed. Molly was getting married and everyone was thrilled . . . except for Molly.

One day, as Molly was assembling the invitations with her mother, a truthful moment erupted; original feelings demanded a voice and Molly began screaming at her mother.

"I cannot do this! I cannot marry Michael! I don't love him . . . you do!" Molly found the truth of her voice. Or maybe I should say the truth of her voice finally found her.

She called off the wedding. She moved out from her parents' home. She found a job and . . . she reattached to her voice, her experience.

It took courage and a readiness to risk her relationship with her parents to reclaim her life, her moment and her identity.

As time passed, the shame and disgrace of Molly canceling the wedding subsided for the Cooks. In time, Molly met a man she found to be her perfect match. True to form for this family, he didn't come with the right ingredients for her parents and until this day, the Cooks don't know what Molly sees in him. But, Molly is happy, with her man, with her choices, with her life's path and with herself.

We all find our truth in the intentions of our feelings. Whether our parents, or society in general force us away from those truths, they still remain inside of us. We either have to stand up and rebel from the agenda being forced, or we have to live hiding our true feelings, our true experience in order to keep peace ("Going underground.")

You have no idea how prevalent this phenomenon is in our families today. Neither option is healthy or necessary! Parents can learn to honor and protect the true experience of their child . . . while guiding, coaching, and loving them through the experience.

Parents can set a culture of expectations and standards for their child to live within without forcing them to detach from their feelings, or hide their truth.

Parents can accept their child and the "voice" inside them without abandoning their standards for themselves or the family environment they create.

Building self-esteem in our children is more about believing in them rather than believing in your picture of them.

When Dr. Spock talked about promoting positive self-esteem through successful performance over 60 years ago, it sounded wonderful to everyone. Little did he or any of us know that society would ultimately define success as anything but failure. The positive affirmation of success actually became the judgment of anything outside the parents "picture of success." Take a deep breathe and relax now.

Now you understand why I apologized in the beginning of Chapter Two . . . This was a lot to absorb.

. . . You know, I never did quite understand what "Beam me up Scotty" had to do with positive self-image. Oh wait . . . that's the *other* Spock! . . . Never mind.

CHAPTER THREE

Going Underground

" **S**uccess at any and all cost" brings with it the potential for dishonesty, for short cuts, for hiding ones truth and for "GOING UNDER-GROUND!"

We all find our truth in the intention of our feelings. Whether or not our parents or society in general force us away from those truths in order to "perform" a certain way, the truths still remain inside of us.

We either have to "stand up" to the agenda being forced upon us and fight to have our "voice" heard, OR we live our lives hiding our true feelings in order to keep peace. To keep that peace or to simply get through the moment, we take our true feelings, thoughts, decisions and actions and GO UNDER-GROUND while portraying a "picture" consistent with the agenda of our parents.

Going underground is that process of DETACHING from the feelings of the moment we are in, (our truth) while ATTACHING our thoughts to whatever vigilance it takes to portray the "picture" of the agenda for our parents. It is disingenuous and illusionary.

"Pulling off" the illusion for our parents and then living a different reality "underground" becomes the ultimate goal for emotional survival.

Every human needs to have the freedom to feel their moment and express their position safely.

How could we possibly know what our own original feelings are, when we are putting on an act that represents one person to our parents while we are truly living another reality?

What then is true about our relationship with our parents? What then, is true about our relationship with ourselves? And what happens to our self-esteem when the premise of why we go underground is that our true voice just isn't good enough for our parents?

What can the feeling for a child be when their voice is not respected or welcome by the most influential persons in their world?

What can the feeling that a child has when they lose respect in their own voice and give up the effort of fighting for its worth? The child must abandon their own integrity and disconnect from the truthful experience, just so that they can cope surviving in someone else's agenda.

It is more than unhealthy to live your life comfortably lying in order to keep peace, and in order to keep people off your back. Ultimately, it becomes emotionally dangerous to do what you wish without regard for how it may affect someone else. (See Tiger Woods, Ben Roethlesberger, or Bill Clinton.) And we are living with generations of young adults raised in this paradigm while living in a society that seems to tolerate it.

I met Peter Robinson, his two brothers and his parents in family counseling many years ago. The Robinsons are a very close knit family. They spent a lot of time with each other through many sporting events. You see, the boys were all great athletes in high school.

Mr. and Mrs. Robinson had high praise for their boys' accomplishments in both sports and academics. They were proud of all three sons. The goal was that when it was time for each son to graduate high school, they would be positioned nicely to go off to good universities, and maybe even play their sport on a college level. The family looked great. The parents felt great! The parents had a clear view of what they expected from their boys and each boy followed the agenda to a tee. Philanthropy, church, community, athletics, family, strong work ethic; these were the values in the foundation of the Robinsons and the boys embraced them wholeheartedly.

So, why then were the Robinsons sitting in my office on a cold wintry night looking for guidance? As this was the last family I would expect to see. By the way, they were the last family that ever thought they would seek me out.

Why then? Because Peter, their oldest was going off to college soon and he wasn't "himself" lately. He was being "completely disrespectful" to his father and his attitude toward all those values he once embraced were now a struggle for him.

"On drugs?" Proposed his mother. "Too big for his britches! Just a real punk!" Replied his dad. Peter's response . . . silence!

His brothers became his spokesmen and they made his case for "being fine."

"Senior-itis was the unanimous conclusion by everyone on Peter's behalf. Everyone except, you guessed it . . . Me!

You see, there was no room for anyone's voice in the family except Dad, (a very common phenomenon, I'm afraid.) Even my voice had no value, unless I agreed with Dad's conclusion that Peter was just frustrated with high school and ready to graduate. I was getting paid here to give my opinion, I made a strong case that we try NOT to speak for Peter and find a process that would encourage Peter to communicate for himself. I made an even stronger case for the need for Peter to look at HIS feelings and thoughts about his parents' agenda for him and his ideas for himself.

Mr. and Mrs. Robinson ignored my statements as if nothing had been suggested at all. The Robinsons made it perfectly clear to me and to Peter that he needed to "shut his mouth" and get back to being the "great kid" he used to be.

I began to feel (possibly) a little bit like Peter. How frustrating it is to have no voice, no matter how compelling your "case" or opinion may be! When parents go "deaf" on their child's voice, their child feels worthless and devalued. Plain and simple.

SIDE NOTE . . . Boy, did Mr. Robinson remind me of my own father when I was young! Not necessarily in looks but certainly in attitude!

If you don't feel valued for what you think and what you feel, especially about your own experience, how can you possibly feel anything? Peter and I knew that what was inside of him, his true feelings about his experience, his view of himself, all were bursting at the seams. Yet, he opted to shove it far down and live the picture required of him. After all, he was leaving for college soon enough. Peter was headed to Ohio State University in the fall. He actually had no choice. His father, mother, uncles and cousins all went there. (He was in love with Miami University (in Ohio) which would be considered treason in this family.)

By the way, no one knew that little tidbit of information until six years later! Let me explain . . . I said goodbye to the Robinsons after two family sessions (or should I say Mr. Robinson said goodbye to me.) He got what he came for . . . Peter "shut his mouth."

Six years later I received an emergency phone call from Mrs. Robinson. Before I knew it, Peter and his parents were back in my office, and all three were in tears. We all looked a little older and Peter had "filled out" and matured physically as one would between 18 and 24 years of age. So what happened here?

Peter graduated from Ohio State University. He majored in business with a minor in alcohol and women. On graduation morning, he was so hung over that his middle brother had to find him, wake him, dress him and get him to commencement, while his parents and grandparents were unsuspectingly sitting in the audience. Peter made it just in time and "walked" without incident. His brother was scolded by his father for "disappearing." His brother sat down next to Grandma in silence.

Peter went directly from college graduation to Europe for a summer of youth hostiles, alcohol and, of course, women. He packed up his SUV and moved to Philadelphia and entered a prestigious law school that fall. Life was promising for the eldest Robinson son and the picture was falling into perfect view for his parents. His brother next in line was doing well at Ohio State and his youngest brother was a senior at the same private high school all the Robinson boys had attended. Mr. Robinson could not have been happier.

As for Peter, he absolutely loved Philadelphia, his new apartment and his new law school friends. He loved it all so much, that Peter stayed there between school years and spent the summers working in Philadelphia. He received a great clerkship at a law firm for the summer between his first and second year of law school.

The Robinsons had so much pride and touted Peter as an example for his two younger brothers as to how to leap successfully from one level of living to the next. The Robinson family was on cruise control.

One day, during Peter's spring semester of his second year of law school, Peter's grandfather died. The Robinsons called Peter to inform him and to make arrangements for him to come home for the funeral.

They called his house phone, no answer. They called his cell phone, no answer. Cell phones were just gaining popularity then although they were still as big as a small transistor radio.

In an attempt to find their son, Mrs. Robinson called the law school to see if they could pull Peter from his class so that they can make their arrangements. Mrs. Robinson spoke with the secretary in the main office who politely transferred her to the Dean of the law school.

With all the chaos surrounding the death of her father-in-law, she might not have wondered then why she was being transferred to the Dean for such an ordinary request.

With confusion and sympathy, the dean calmly announced to Mrs. Robinson that Peter had quit law school after his first semester there. He had not been a student of their law school for over one year!

Let's have moment of silence here. Sit back, breathe deeply, and take in the magnitude of what you just read. BIG SIGH . . . let's continue with our story . . .

The reality was that Peter Robinson moved to Philadelphia, rented an apartment, entered law school, and dropped out four months later. And he told nobody. Talk about going underground! He had been living there under an illusion of being a law student for the 15 months! THERE WAS NO LAW SCHOOL. THERE WAS NO CLERKSHIP. THERE WAS ONLY ILLUSION!

So what was Peter's truth? Peter Robinson hated school. He felt hatred toward his father. And he felt NOTHING about living a lie and pretending to be a student for as long as the ride would last. He knew that one day he would have to fess up. But that didn't matter. For the time being, he was free to do whatever he wanted, EXCEPT to live with integrity and truthfulness, although that didn't seem to be on his radar.

Underground, Peter lived a great life of sleeping late, playing with his dog, working at a local coffee house part time, and, you guessed it . . . alcohol and women.

Peter Robinson did not, could not and would not share HIS truth with his parents.

So . . . he went WAY underground and created an elaborate illusion of his identity that he nurtured along with tales of law school experiences. And his parents bought it all "hook, line and sinker."

Why? Because the stories fit the picture and the picture fit their agenda. There was no need to question their son. He was a good boy who followed the family culture to a tee. Remember?

Mrs. Robinson sat silently in shock and terror. After what seemed like forever, she finally thanked the dean and hung up the phone.

Now what? How does she tell Peter's father? WHAT does she tell Peter's father?

And when?

Peter finally returned his mother's phone call, with a tale of forgetting his phone back at his apartment as he was sitting in a lecture on family law. Mrs. Robinson could not respond and just softly told Peter that his grandfather had died and what his travel plans for the funeral were going to be.

The Robinsons had a huge memorial service at their church for Mr.

Robinson's father. Hundreds of guests in attendance paid their respects and complimented Peter and his parents for his law school success. Mrs. Robinson simply smiled.

Peter flew back to Philadelphia after the funeral to get back to "school." Mrs. Robinson was now left with the burden of this underground truth and the need to expose it. She waited another week to let life get back to normal. Mr. Robinson was dealing with his own grief, so he barely noticed how awkward his wife was behaving.

You see, the emotional burden of going underground eventually will bleed out to all that are involved . . . even to those who contribute to the child's need to go underground in the first place.

Remember what I said before, **"The feelings of our experience that we detach from for the agenda of someone else never go away."** At some point, we are forced to deal with them.

Everyone must deal not just with the truth of their underground decisions but with the truth of their feelings that have led them there. At some point, every parent will have to face the truth of their child as well. (More on that later.)

Mr. Robinson was more than livid. He was broken. He wondered, who was this person he called his eldest son? What else were they going to uncover? Drugs, perhaps? Gambling, maybe? Prostitution, for God's sake? Lies, lies and more lies! For the Robinsons, there had to be a justification for this type of betrayal. Not once did Mr. Robinson think that maybe, just maybe, the dynamics of his relationship with his eldest son contributed to any of this. Why would he?

Peter chose not to fight for his truth. If you recall, he chose to detach and go silent even in my office six years prior. For him, going underground was so much easier. Think of the emptiness inside of Peter, in order to justify this to himself.

Mr. and Mrs. Robinson flew to Philadelphia. They arrived at Peter's apartment unannounced around 1:00 p.m. on a Tuesday, and rang the doorbell.

Peter opened the door, locked eyes with his father and they both wept uncontrollably for hours.

There was so much to talk about, so much to unravel, so much to confront. Yet, they mentioned nothing and began packing in silence as if everyone knew what to do. For the first time in Peter's life, his father had nothing to say, no condemnation, no editorial comments, and no words of judgment. Mr. Robinson said nothing and it almost drove Peter crazy.

Peter played out this moment in his mind over and over again for 15 months. You see . . . that's what you do when you go underground. You try to predict every consequence. You become "hyper-vigilant" trying to predict every move.

He absolutely expected more of the same "reaction" from his father that he had counted on his whole life; the very same reactions Peter blamed for everything he ever chose to go underground about.

So why were the Robinsons back in my office? Because they really had no choice. It was time to explore the truth of the damage that was done by years of illusions and going underground.

The Robinsons are well meaning people and like most of us, have been taught to set the standard high, and fit our children into a picture and expect them to perform accordingly.

Peter is a great young man, smart, attractive, and also well meaning. But when you are so afraid to speak your "voice" and there is no safety in your family dynamic to do so, you have to find a way to survive. You cannot stay in the feeling of your moment comfortably if it is given no room to breathe, no platform to be heard.

Growing up, Peter became frustrated and angry in reaction to his own fear of his father's reaction to him. There was never room for discussion. Peter either went to war with his dad, or went underground with his feelings, thoughts, decisions and actions. He tried both through the years and underground just seemed less toxic.

For all of those who choose to create an illusion over their own truth, they live with a premise that is quite frightening . . . that they are not worthy of their own voice and that there is no space "above ground" for their thoughts and decisions based on their feelings. Say goodbye to your self-worth and self-esteem.

Peter's life of illusion could only be accomplished by abandoning a fundamental characteristic of his conscience . . . his integrity. He may have betrayed his parents, BUT he abandoned himself! You see, Peter based his entire ability to function underground on what was truly the illusion . . . the trust between he and his parents.

His parents would deposit his tuition and living expenses into his checking account, assuming he was paying his tuition and expenses for law school. Ultimately, he STOLE just under ONE HUNDRED THOUSAND DOLLARS from his own mother and father!

Maybe we should take another moment of silence here as we reflect on the magnitude of this . . . $100,000! How might you handle this, if it happened to you? Because, it easily could be any one of us!

The Robinsons were clearly broken. Their picture of their family was shattered and their trust in Peter was gone. Mr. Robinson could not lay his eyes on Peter as we all sat in my office. Everyone was in tears, including me. The story was huge. The betrayal was even larger.

What I found quite troubling was Peter's abandonment of his feelings and his ability to do whatever he wanted regardless of who it hurt and the lies necessary to pull it off. His story, frankly, in process, is truly no different than the teenager who tells his mother he is sleeping over at one friend's house, when he is really somewhere else.

I know you are thinking . . . "Are you crazy Phil?" Okay. Calm down and let me explain.

"Are you really comparing a teenager lying about their whereabouts with a kid who for 15 months lived a lie and stole a hundred thousand dollars from his parents to do so?" My answer is a QUALIFIED YES!!!

The process of going underground begins from the same place, regardless of the magnitude of story. When the communication dynamics in the family culture between child and parent inhibits a safe dialogue, the detachment between feeling and thought may occur. When the detachment occurs the growth of the conscience stops. Integrity is at risk.

So, the child then becomes at risk for putting up an illusion while going underground with the truth of their choices. The magnitude of that underground choice is specific to the child, and specific to the process of their development and the circumstances of their life. The illusion of trust is the same here, as the child relies on that illusion to support their underground decisions.

I know what you are thinking now . . . . Doesn't every kid do this a little bit?

And the answer is . . . it doesn't have to be that way. There is a difference between "testing" the family culture and completely abandoning it.

We call "testing the family culture" growing up, or adolescence; the process of testing the messages you are growing up with in order to differentiate your own identity from your parents. Normal, right?

However, when the process center of the conscience detaches rather than slows down, as in adolescence, the underground behavior replaces the process of testing the limits with IGNORING the limits. There lacks a complete conscience with the detachment that is not normal to child development. Detachment from your feelings is a much more dangerous place to be.

Think of the possibilities if we are communicating in a way that supports and promotes the voice of our children while guiding their expectations with love and nurturance. Think of the possibilities if we live in a culture that does not tolerate justifying the absence of integrity. Think of a life experience where the standards by which we live, and hold ourselves accountable to is communicated without judgment to our children . . . allowing all of us to live truthfully "ABOVE GROUND."

I am not naive here. I don't believe that we can ever move our culture far enough from where we have descended so that we will live completely in integrity.

However, I do believe we MUST stop justifying how we live, how we continue to do things, and the lessening of standards we have allowed for ourselves and our children.

And so, I encouraged Peter to break his silence. It was time for Peter to share not only the truth of his underground decisions but the truth of his feelings that led him there.

Mr. Robinson was truly broken. He didn't even try to take control. But he wasn't very interested in listening to his son's feelings either.

As Peter began to talk, his father began to erupt and his mother began to sob. I forced Peter to continue and push through his parents' reactions and finish what he wanted to say.

Something Peter said abruptly halted both parents' reactions. They were finally listening. What came out of Peter's mouth was that he NEVER wanted to do any of it. No sports, no school work, no philanthropy, none of it.

"Who are you then? What did we ever do to you to have you do this to us?" his mother asked in a whimper.

And then the light went on and Peter proceeded to take the next two hours venting his feelings about his parents, particularly his dad.

Mr. Robinson looked over at me defeated and asked, "What do we do now? He clearly hates us."

"No, Mr. Robinson. No, Peter doesn't hate you. Peter hates Peter for never finding a way to think like you, or feel like you, thus failing to please you," I demanded.

In a weird way, if Peter didn't go underground, he felt he would have lost his parents forever. Going underground kept them in his life, at least temporarily.

The Robinsons met with Peter and me on a regular basis for another year. They needed to get to know their son . . . for the first time at 24-years-old.

Peter in turn had to SHARE Peter honestly with his parents without altering himself in fear of their reaction. They also set up a plan for Peter to repay the $100,000 realistically over time. It was Peter's initiation. We are never too old to develop our conscience.

Going underground is so prevalent today and often justified by what we consider "normal" development. The truth is that we as parents must find a way to communicate safely. Parents must encourage the voice of their children and keep the family dynamics "above ground" by allowing for the feelings, thoughts and opinions to be welcome into the family culture.

Not every child will make decisions as detached and illusionary as Peter Robinson's. But if we can learn from The Robinsons' experience, we learn that truth is indeed not perception. Truth is the facts without judgment.

In the next chapter, we need to make a departure from all this for just a few minutes and talk about PERFORMANCE. We must make sure we understand what role performance plays in our expectations of our children.

This will be just enough performance theory for our purposes to understand where it fits in the change in attitude that I am asking parents to make.

So, I will leave you, for now, with thoughts from my own teenage experience. In 1970, the great Cat Stevens wrote a popular song called, "Father and Son." As a 13-year-old boy, I related so intensely to the lyrics of this song that it essentially became my personal anthem for my teenage years.

He sang of the struggle between a young man's true voice and the agenda his father had for him. As the song tells us, the young man's only solution to his conflict between who he "was" and who he "was supposed to be" was to "go away" somewhere . . . anywhere!

In 1977, Cat Stevens walked away from being a pop culture icon. He became Yosuf Islam. Going Underground . . . Maybe? Living his truth . . . Perhaps.

GOING UNDERGROUND
A Poem By Phil Dembo

I remember being told that
    the world was looking at me.
I remember feeling the pain
    of what that meant.
I remember never trying
    as hard as they wanted me to.
I remember sitting silently,
    wishing I could vent.

I gave them everything
    they asked for.
I gave them the picture
    that they painted.
I gave them very little
    of the truth of who I am.
I gave them a picture
    that was tainted.

I survived my life
    by going underground.
I survived my life
    while feeling so lost.
I survived my life
    by losing my integrity.
I survived by going underground,
    at such a painful cost.

CHAPTER FOUR

Performance

I
t was 1989 and it was an unusually cool, late summer day in our hometown of St. Louis, (an odd occurrence around here since the weather is typically humid and hot that time of year.)

My daughter, Elizabeth was going to enter kindergarten in the fall. She was a bright, beautiful little girl (still is, just not so little . . . she's 27!) and was so very excited about making new friends, learning and having fun!

Lizzy (Elizabeth's nickname) and I were walking through the mall on that cool summer day when we ran into Mrs. Betty Schwartz, the assistant superintendent of the school district Lizzy was about attend. I knew Mrs. Schwartz through various connections both professionally and personally, and we both always said hello when we would see one another.

As Mrs. Schwartz approached us, I explained to Lizzy who she was and Lizzy became playfully animated. My daughter, like her father, enjoyed people very much and would chat with anyone who would chat with her.

"Hi, my name is Lizzy Dembo and I'm going to your school soon!" she said with her big "Lizzy" smile!

"Hello, Lizzy. My name is Mrs. Schwartz and I am so happy to meet you!"

"ARE YOU READY TO COMPETE WHEN YOU COME TO MY SCHOOL THIS FALL?""

Eeeerrrrrrrr . . . (Enter sound effect of wheels screeching to a halt!!!) I couldn't believe what I had just heard. Did I miss something? Surely, Mrs. Schwartz said . . . "Are you ready to have FUN?" Or "MAKE FRIENDS" Or "LEARN" Or anything . . . but COMPETE!" Lizzy was five-years-old for God's sake! The word she used, she meant . . . "COMPETE!"

I remember that moment as if it were yesterday. I knew that the school district Betty Schwartz ran was a nationally recognized district and was very well respected but I didn't realize at what cost. The standard of success for a school district back in 1989 was rated so high due to the competitive nature of its students. And sadly, today, it hasn't gotten any better.

Success at all and any cost began in kindergarten for my daughter, and there wasn't a thing that I could do about it! My hope was that maybe what I created at home in our family culture would balance this intensity and stress for her. As a parent, what else could I do? I couldn't change the culture of the school district by her first day of kindergarten! (More on that concept in the next chapter.)

Today, the philosophy of competition and performance begins at birth and takes off in preschool or daycare. The pressure of making sure your child "wins" at everything they do and is able to keep up with (compete with) their peers is overwhelmingly stressful for parents.

When did we as a society go from HUMAN BEINGS to HUMAN DOERS to HUMAN PERFORMERS?

Do you remember in Chapter Two we discussed that based upon the philosophies of the 50s, 60s, and 70s, parents today are taught to build success for their child as the only permissible outcome? The goal of this model was to build a positive self-esteem in our child, not an identity unable to feel the process of life or deal with outcomes other than successful ones.

Well, in 1989, that was Betty Schwartz's version of building my daughter's (and her classmates') self-esteem by readying her to compete, and thus by definition, fight to win! Twenty-two years later, competition is everywhere. Performance is so woven into our thinking that winning and success have become one in the same.

So if building our child's self-esteem is about providing them with successful experiences as Dr. Spock taught us years ago, then today winning has become the only option to that end.

There is one major problem with the progression of his theory into today's working model . . . WHERE THERE IS A WINNER, THERE MUST BE A LOSER! And remember . . . losing is failure . . . and failure is impermissible.

Performance is the standard that parents today have for their children. Performance is the "brush" that paints the "picture" parents have for their child, in large part because it is the paintbrush society has all of us utilize today in order to paint our own success.

"Competing to be the best" seems to be the only goal, and the actual experience of the EFFORT and PROCESS it takes to perform seems much less important.

This is where we are truly at risk.

If effort and the process of trying isn't valued or experienced, AND the outcome of winning is at all cost, it leaves open the possibility that parents and children both will do anything for the win. Anything, regardless of the consequence.

Conflict and lack of balance in the home; stress and anxiety in our children; "going underground," and abandonment of integrity are all very real consequences of our performance-based win at any and all cost culture.

"Soccer mom," for example, is an endearing term of the times that describes the phenomenon we are speaking of here. It is now permissible for our child to be at school all day long, come home, get ready and go off to soccer practice (or any other sport or activity for that matter,) all evening long, two, three, four times or more a week. Dinners are often eaten in the van, on the run and out of a bag.

What could possibly be so compelling, so important about after school activities, that parents are willing to give up a balanced schedule, a balanced diet, a balanced experience for their child or themselves, in order to do what? Play soccer?

The truth is . . . parents think *everyone* is doing it so my child must do it too. To compete and win, our children must keep up with what everyone else is doing or they will lag behind and have no chance of success . . . athletically, academically, and socially. That's the fear. That's the stress. That's the culture we have chosen to accept.

This discussion is not just about sports per se, it's about everything in our lives. Somehow, with this belief system that winning and success are one in the same, and that success is essential for self-esteem, everything our children may choose must be judged as performance and forced into a picture of success parents create for them.

Therefore, parents will choose for the child to make sure that the child is in tandem with "everyone else." Pictures created by parents and society CANNOT be more important than the truth of your child. If it is, you will risk the healthy development of their self-esteem and identity. If by chance, a parent's "picture" and the child's truth are one in the same . . . that's awesome! But what if they are not?

Not every child is a great athlete. Not every child is a great student. Not every child is a great talent. Not every child is comfortable fitting into the picture someone else may have for them. Yet parents are so afraid to see their child as that "individual" separate from the scripted picture.

To be an individual in this model of thinking is to be judged as "different" than everybody else, which is seen as failure, and again, failure is impermissible!

How unfortunate for the child and the parent! This creates so much pressure for the parents to demand the picture and so much pressure for the child to either fit the picture, or react to it.

Today, from birth on and throughout life, this judgment exists and the comparison to others is constant.

HERE'S THE IRONY . . . SUCCESSFUL PERFORMANCE RE-QUIRES NO JUDGMENT! (Just like effective parenting, by the way! More on that in the next chapter as well.)

I told you at the end of last chapter, we needed to visit Performance Theory for just a minute, and this is why. We are doing this all wrong!

Society expects us to perform to win. **Wrong.**

Our children today are parented to perform. **Wrong.**

Performance today is judged by outcome. **Wrong.**

And parents are "schlepping" their children day and night, franticly trying to keep up with "everyone else" . . . **Absolutely Wrong!**

(Okay, I know. A little judgment of my own is going on here. Hey, I live in the same world you do. Don't I?)

PERFORMANCE, by definition, **is the process of portraying ones effort and intention to try.** The performer must NOT concern himself with the judgment of others. If he does, he alters the process of his effort by the truth of his intention. Intention to give effort is absolutely different than the intention to win.

The intention of performance MUST be to portray effort without concern in that moment, for anything else but the experience of the process. So, performance is about effort in the moment without concern for outcome.

If we stay in the moment of our effort and our process, outcome will take care of itself. We feel the process of our effort (experience) and assume the outcome will follow the process. By the way . . . it always does!

I know many of you are freaking out right now, but please be patient with me.

You're confused, as I would be if I were you, and probably asking yourself, "What the hell is he talking about?"

"Performance must be about outcome, otherwise, why perform at all?" Boy, is *that* the million dollar question! Isn't it? "Why perform at all?"

We have evolved into a society where process means very little and WINNING MEANS EVERYTHING. (Today, kids frequently stop trying if they don't think they can win. Participating for the sake of the experience now has very little value in our society.) Performance as an experience cannot be judged on its outcome because outcome may be circumstantial to the true experience. Focusing on the judgment of the outcome ALTERS our intention to try, and the true experience of our effort.

Performance must ONLY be about the intention to try and the process of that effort or we experience nothing, we feel nothing and we learn nothing about ourselves.

Please, remember . . . every experience begins with a feeling of intention. We must keep that process safe to keep the integrity of the effort in tact. (Are you noticing yet, the correlation between the performance theory we are talking about here and conscience development in our child we discussed in Chapter Two?) Maybe a short story could help right about now . . .

Sylvia Howard is an 80-year-old woman who I visit with periodically in my office. She is simply awesome. Sylvia has been a widow for 15 years now and has transitioned into her life alone very well. She has many friends and participates in all kinds of activities. She entertains often, travels frequently and continues to be a very active golfer.

Let's reflect for a moment . . . Given that my own mother passed away at 82-years-old after being ill for 10 years and bedridden for her last five, I find Sylvia to be a truly lucky lady.

Sylvia and her husband were very successful financially throughout their lives together. They had been active members of an exclusive country club for most of their marriage. In fact, Sylvia is still very active there today. Throughout the years of her membership, she has held many leadership positions at this club.

One year, while in her 40's, Sylvia Howard was elected the chairwoman of the coveted Annual Lady's Golf Tournament. This is one of the highest honors a woman can be given at this particular club. Sylvia showed great leadership and a record number of women played in the tournament that year, which was a true testament of Sylvia's popularity. The event was a shining success.

At the end of each golf season, which is early September (around these parts,) the country club holds one final golf tournament for the current and former chairwomen of the tournament. It is truly a lovely golfing event in honor of these great leaders of the club, followed by a beautiful luncheon. Sylvia Howard has participated in this honorary tournament every year since her turn at the helm. She loves this event and it is quite an honor for her.

Now, Sylvia is quite the golfer as well, and she loves to play. She also loves to judge herself by her winning and losing record. She sees it as her "motivator." After all, she learned judgment just like the rest of us.

She judges so much so, that the process of playing has become more and more stressful and less enjoyable, as her skills have weakened due to her aging. She has become even more critical of herself as she has gotten older . . . driven to maintain the "picture" of Sylvia she believes her world expects.

In golf, the lower your score, the better your performance. Or should I say . . . "the better your outcome."

Sylvia played in this year's honorary tournament at the age of 80. She also "shot an 80" for her total score for the tournament. It was her lowest score in five years. Sylvia Howard "won" the tournament with the lowest total score. She was so very pleased with herself. Sort of. She was definitely the talk of the luncheon that followed.

However, there was one nagging issue for Sylvia Howard . . . Emily Swanson.

Emily Swanson was sick at home with the flu that weekend and had to withdraw from the tournament. Emily Swanson is a very good golfer and had won this event the last three years with scores of 76, 74, and 79 respectively.

Sylvia couldn't let go of her own judgment and feel the truth of her own experience. She shot an 80 for the tournament and that's the "what is." BUT . . . had Emily played, would the 80 have stood up? That's a case of the anxiety and fear of "what might have been."

Sylvia Howard struggles with the "what is" and justifies her life by "what might have been." (Many of us do!)

Had Emily Swanson played in this year's tournament, Sylvia believes wholeheartedly that Emily would have won. More importantly to Sylvia, she believes that "everyone else" believes that as well! (There's that "everyone else" judgment thing rearing its ugly head again!)

So, winning is everything, right? Sylvia won, right? And yet its still not good enough for her! There is always the circumstance that she can create in her mind that devalues her accomplishment.

Why? Because winning is NOT where the value of our experience lies, but yet we believe it does. It lies in the intention to try and the feelings of the experience of our effort. So, in our culture, winning is everything, feeling the moment is not valued, detachment must be inevitable. We fill the void of that detachment with fear, anxiety and ultimately judgment. (This is exactly why parents must stop judging their children and embrace their individuality.)

Remember, where there is a winner, there is a loser. And losing cannot be judged as a fate worse than death. Losing (failure) is a possible outcome of the process of effort; no different than winning. If we value the intention to try and the effort in our actions, whatever the outcome, we will feel the value of our experience and continually improve our process.

Without judgment, no effort or experience is big or small, it just is "what it is." We can evaluate our effort factually and make adjustments accordingly. If we truly value the process we are in, we will embrace our effort, embrace our experience, and not be too afraid to fail.

Sylvia shot an 80 for the tournament. The score had an outcome of "winning" without Emily Swanson in attendance. The same score with Emily participating may have had a same outcome. But, it also may NOT have. Had Sylvia played with the same intention to try, with no judgment of the circumstance (she had no control over that anyway,) the experience of the process resulting in the score of 80, is where she would find the value of her experience, with or without Emily Swanson. Sylvia would have enjoyed every swing, every hole, every bit of the sunshine and scenery of the golf course she so dearly loved. **Sylvia's experience was in the feeling of her moment, not the outcome of her score.**

The score then only reflects an outcome of her experience, nothing more. And her "win" only reflects circumstantially, an outcome of her score as it relates to the field of other participants.

Sylvia could not feel satisfied in her efforts, regardless of the outcome or circumstance, because she detached herself from what really mattered . . . the feelings of the experience itself. She replaced that with the anxiety and judgment of winning, and losing and what she thinks other people think of her.

You see, Sylvia, like the rest of us, only has control over her own efforts, her own feelings, her own execution of her skills and her own process. There is a "truth" in that! The outcome of that "truth" resulted in her lowest score in years. Yet she could never feel pleased, because performance for her is attached to the outcome of winning and the perception others have of her.

Sylvia, literally couldn't "win for trying" and couldn't even "win for winning."

Phew . . . simply exhausting!

. . . Side note to ponder with regard to all of this . . .

I have always loved the sport of swimming or track as great models for the understanding of performance. As a swimmer, for example, you race against yourself and no one else, really. Each time you race, your goal is to swim faster than your best previous time. Like Sylvia's score of 80, your best time may win the race, or place you fifth, depending on who is racing with you and their times.

Conversely, your worst time in years may win the race as well. Great swimmers focus their intention on swimming faster, and letting the outcome be whatever the outcome will be. Hours and hours of preparation, practice, and effort in the pool has only one intention . . . to be faster than the time before; to better themselves through the intention to try! It is truly the only thing they have any control over.

I have been very fortunate in my career to have worked with this issue of PERFORMANCE with high school, college, and professional athletes. Inherent in the theory of performance is the foundation of "Truth Without Judgment."

Great athletes understand that there is a truth in their intention to try, and a truth in their portrayal of that effort. (Performance is the portrayal of one's effort.)

Professional athletes understand that once they indulge themselves with judgment of the outcome of their efforts, their intention changes and their performance changes as a result. No longer is their intention to feel the process of their experience. Now their intention alters its focus on the outcome at any and all cost.

Let me tell you about Brad Bentley . . .

Brad was a highly touted punter from a major college football program. He was in the top five in all statistical categories, nationally for college punters. He was a third round NFL draft pick in April, 2010.

Brad Bentley, by the way, is a wonderful young man from a very stable, loving family. Brad is just "plain good people." His dream, like many young men, was to one day be an NFL Football player.

It was so exciting for he and his family to hear his name called on draft day and know that his dream was about to come true.

Brad was drafted in April, graduated in May, and moved in June to Tampa, Florida, the city of his new employer. There is no security and no stability for NFL punters and their signing bonus money is not nearly what other positions command. Don't get me wrong . . . it's a great gig if you can get it. Brad's $100,000 signing bonus is nothing to sneeze at. It's just in a different league as compared to the millions of dollars given to athletes joining the NFL in the other positions on the team.

Brad was living his dream though. He was now an NFL punter. Training camp and the NFL preseason was underway. Brad was learning the culture and finding his place on the team as a rookie. He was so excited and anxiously ready for his first pre-season action. It was a home game, so all his friends and family were in attendance to cheer him on.

Because the game was "preseason," it had no real meaning because it didn't count on the team's official record. But for Brad Bentley, as well as for all the rookies on the team, it meant everything.

As the game unfolded, Brad was ready for action. He has a "large leg" and he was ready to show it off. ("Large leg" in football terms means having a strong and powerful kick.)

Quickly into the game, Brad was called on to punt the ball away. The ball was snapped, Brad caught it and punted it off the side of his foot. He "pooched" it.

His first punt of his NFL career, and he pooched it!

Okay, let's take a moment for a lesson in football language: You now know the meaning of a large leg. A POOCHED PUNT is when a punter misses the ball cleanly and it doesn't travel far and deep into the back of the playing field. The goal of all punters is to kick the ball as far and deep as the coach asks him to, with enough "HANG TIME" (flying time in the air) to let his teammates run to the ball and tackle the player from the other team who catches his punt. Back to Brad's pooched punt . . . .

Panic filled his body, judgment filled his mind. The picture of his first punt in the NFL was nothing like he had imagined. He could not wait until his next opportunity to PROVE that his pooch was just a fluke. (judgment, judgment, judgment – and all of himself.)

As he ran off the field, his coach yelled, "Bentley, shrug it off and get ready for the next time!"

His next opportunity came quickly and Brad was going to "bomb" this one! (Oh, sorry, I forgot . . . "BOMB" means to kick it way high and far.) He ran out onto the field for his next opportunity and he kicked the sh#% out of the ball! And it pooched to the right side and traveled only five yards. Boos filled the stadium and for Brad Bentley, his NFL dream became his worst nightmare!

What was going wrong? This kid was one of the best punters in college and was just drafted for God's sake?

Remember, I said earlier that judgment alters one's intention to try and portray effort (perform.) Brad abandoned the process of his experience and detached from the feeling of his punting moment. He replaced his process (something he has done a million times since he was 13-years-old) with panic and judgment of himself. His new intention was NOT to follow the process he has done so well for so long, but to PROVE himself with each and every punt. No longer was he comfortable with himself. No longer was he feeling the moment of his process. No longer was he able to portray his efforts (perform) as he had countless times before in his career. No longer was Brad an NFL punter!

Brad Bentley was "cut" (dismissed) from the team that drafted him and he did not play again that season. He is currently working at a Sports Authority in his home town, waiting for another opportunity.

He is also working on being fully in the moment of his process of punting, without judgment. You see, punting on a practice field, punting in a try-out with an NFL team, or punting in the Super Bowl are all the same punts. They have to be or we cannot stay in the moment of our experience. No punt can be too large or too small.

If Brad learns to stay in the moment of the experience of his punting process, and kick the ball the same way he has for years, his consistency will be reliable and his performance will be as well. Then, he never has to replace the feeling of his kick with the feeling of "proving" himself again.

Performance, on any stage in life requires skill, discipline, consistency, practice, process and acceptance of the truth without judgment.

. . . Please pause here and read that last sentence again . . . thanks!

Brad was no longer a punter on the field. He was too focused on his judgment and on proving himself to ever JUST BE HIMSELF.

I recognize that humans are not machines and have feelings about moments that are not performed as practiced. But stepping out of the process that holds the skills you rely on, the consistency you have developed and the intention to follow a process you feel comfortable in, only puts you AT RISK of completing the very performance you are attempting to portray . . . You might want to read that last sentence again as well.

Detaching from the experience that has defined you in a panic to prove yourself ABANDONS the very identity that defines you in the first place.

Success does not define self-esteem. self-esteem is defined by one's effort and intention to try.

I asked you earlier whether you saw the correlation between this discussion on performance and our previous discussion on developing the conscience as we raise our children. I believe that every great life needs a great coach. Each parent is that great coach a child needs to partner with, in order to effectively practice their intention to try and portray their effort.

A great coach (parent) believes in the truth of their athlete (child) and guides, teaches, gives advice and notices things that the athlete may not.

Coaches (parents) teach the athlete (child) to look at the facts without judgment and strategize how to adjust to these facts to maximize the experience. But, they don't play the game for the athlete. Coaches stand on the sidelines and let the athlete play.

It isn't the coaches "picture" of the athlete that's relevant; it's the athletes truth on the field that matters most.

Parents are the coaches for their child's life. They provide the practice field, the rules of the game, the strategies and discipline to train, and the love and support to keep practicing. But it's the child who is the athlete of their own experience. It is the child who has to get out there on the field of their life, practice and perform. Parents need to stay on the sidelines to coach and affirm.

CHAPTER FIVE

Responsive Parenting . . . Truth Without Judgment

I recognize I have asked you to absorb a depth of information without giving you any real guidance toward change and a new way of approaching your parenting. THANK YOU for hanging in there with me thus far in our journey together.

Now is the time to begin to pull it all together into something you can adapt to your own lives. Let's focus **less** on what we are doing wrong and talk **more** about what parents CAN do to raise healthy kids who possess a strong sense of themselves and the ability to self-regulate as adults.

"Truth without judgment" refers to the "WHAT IS" rather than the "WHAT SHOULD BE" of an experience. What IS the truth (fact) rather than what SHOULD be the "picture?"

As I have said many times in this book . . . parents today have learned to parent their children based on the "picture" or agenda they have for their child, rather than the child's actual experience. The parent's agenda seems, for the most part, to be a combination of what THEY want for their child and what they feel "EVERYBODY ELSE" pictures for their children.

I have shared stories of families where the dynamics of a parent's agenda can be so rigid that it sends their child "underground." This is a truly common phenomenon in our society today.

I have discussed with you, that the underdevelopment of a child's conscience can be a consequence of a parent's agenda taking priority over the child's own actual experience.

We have also talked about how frightening it can be for parents when their child's individuality is so different than the picture they have for them; OR the picture "everybody else" has for a child in that circumstance, at that age and stage of development.

Who is this "everybody" everybody always refers to anyway? I would sure like to meet these people who seem to have the power to set the cultural norms for (you guessed it,) "everybody else."

Parenting the "truth" of what is, rather than parenting the "picture" of what should be, creates a safety in the dynamics between the parent and the child. To make that shift from the parenting of pictures with judgment to parenting in "truth without judgment" requires a great deal of courage and a great deal of trust in yourself and your child.

Let's establish some concepts for our new way of thinking . . .

JUDGMENT is the act of taking my "PREFERENCE" and "UNSOLICITLY" assigning it to another person's circumstance, decision, choice or experience.

Every one of us has a preference about something, BUT, NO ONE really has a right to impose that preference onto someone else's experience, UNLESS requested. (That's right, not even on our children!)

I am not talking about the basic set of rules parents are responsible for in keeping their child safe and protected and running their household smoothly. I am not talking about the family culture parents are responsible for creating that impacts a child's experience growing up. I AM talking about OUR preference to control how a child should see the world, feel their experience and make choices based on our picture FOR them.

The world is not so uniform and bland that every child should be expected to behave like every other child of a similar age. These NORMS "everybody" expects a child to adhere to are NOT necessarily a child's feelings of their experience or view of themselves.

JUDGMENT typically comes out of one's fear and insecurity. Parents are so afraid that their child will struggle in life, not have successful outcomes, or be different than "everybody else". Thus, a child is judged before they have a chance to experience something their own way.

The pressure to DEMAND the "picture" as a way to feel safe that our child is headed in the right direction is huge. So as parents feel safe with the "picture" they are expecting they have created an unsafe emotional dynamic for their child.

As we talked about in the beginning of the book, this dynamic interferes with the healthy process of a child's identity development. Parents MUST live with the experience of fear and worry so that their child doesn't have to.

Our children MUST have a PLACE to feel safe to succeed, to fail, to give effort, and to have feelings and an opinion about their own life's experience.

Parents, YOU ARE THAT PLACE!

In parenting, the most commonly used form of judgment is the "comparative analysis." Parents will compare their child to another child, in order to somehow "motivate" (manipulate?) their child. I never understood how this approach could do anything positive for a child's self-esteem. Why would a child feel good about themselves when they are being told that they are not as good as another kid or that they are only good because they are better than another kid? . . . Talk about not being comfortable in your own skin! (Yikes!) So what are parents so afraid of? They are afraid their child isn't good enough and won't perform well enough.

Do you remember in the last chapter, I said to you, "Successful performance requires no judgment?" We were talking then about the PERFORMANCE itself as a place to portray one's effort. We agreed that as a society, we will always have to live with some level of acceptance that performance is unavoidable. Our children, as we are, will be expected to perform on some level throughout their lifetime.

The irony here is that performance, itself, requires no judgment (as parenting does) so that the effort and process can be experienced, without fear of the outcome. Parents expect their child to perform and use judgment as a way to motivate and maximize performance, because the truth is, parents are the ones afraid of the outcome.

Judgment inhibits performance YET children are expected to perform motivated by it. Hmmm, what is wrong with this picture? What then could possibly motivate a child to give effort, if their parent isn't holding a picture for them to fit into? What approach could a parent take in their child's life if they are not there to make sure they fit in that picture "everybody else" has for them? What happened that we lost TRUST in ourselves and our children that we need the picture of "everyone else" to guide our lives, in the first place?

Parents . . . it is time to stop being afraid that your child is so different than "everybody else" and embrace their individuality.

BE A RESPONSIVE PARENT TO YOUR CHILD'S EXPERIENCE.

RESPOND to your child, never REACT.

REACTION is the expression of your feelings WITH your thoughts, emoting and judging. RESPONSE is the expression of your thoughts ABOUT your feelings, (Processing.)

When we react to our child, we emote our feelings and thus, we judge. We impose our preference unsolicited, through our emotions.

How are children supposed to view themselves when they feel judged by their parents? How are children supposed to respond to reactions of judgments by their parents other than to either fight back, or go underground?

(As Cat Stevens wrote . . . *"From the moment I could talk, I was ordered to listen . . ."*)

WHY RESPOND RATHER THAN REACT?

The safety created when communicating responsively allows for a parent to partner with their child. Through this partnership, a parent will be included in on the child's processing of feelings that get interpreted into thoughts that thus become decisions and actions. That's where the courage comes in.

Many times a parent may see the child interpreting their feelings in a way that parents believe may have a negative outcome but must ONLY coach and guide the process, without changing the process. It cannot be the parent's experience. It must be the child's.

FEELING. THOUGHT. DECISION. ACTION . . . This is the process of all experience, and the development of identity comes from one's intention to feel this process. Parents need to "parent" between FEELING and THOUGHT (where the true meaning of the experience lies.) Parents no longer will focus their involvement between THOUGHT and ACTION. (Where we have parented for the last 60 years.)

As we say in the therapy world . . . focus on the "process" rather than the "outcome." Focus on the "intent" of the experience rather than the "content" of the moment. The subject matter is much less important in the scheme of how your child feels about themselves, than the reason why they made the choice to begin with.

"Why" any of us make a decision is much more important to our self-esteem and identity than the decision itself. Let me give you an example of "RESPONSIVE PARENTING."

My son, Justin just turned 21-years-old. He is a junior in college and was recently hired by a hotel near his university. He is working 30 hours per week at their front desk and going to school full time. (He decided to "retire" from college lacrosse and finish school as soon as possible.)

He is living alone in a one bedroom apartment that Linda and I pay for, and is using his earnings for his own spending money. Justin has announced that he is purchasing a puppy.

"After all, Dad, I am making my own spending money!" Justin explained.

(Okay, Phil . . . Time to practice what you preach . . . don't focus on his thoughts; attend to his feelings that lead to these thoughts! Remember . . . RESPOND, don't react!)

"A DOG?" WHAT THE HELL ARE YOU DOING? . . . Just kidding! I wanted to see if you were still awake! It actually went more like this . . .

"A dog? You have really wanted your own dog for a long time, haven't you?" I said, maybe holding my breathe just a little bit. (Courage Phil, courage!)

"Yeah, I have and now that I'm working, I figured out that I can afford it," he replied.

"What brings this up now, Jus?" I asked. (I call him "Jus" playfully . . . short for Justin, of course.)

"Dad, I am so lonely living by myself and most of my friends still play lacrosse so either I don't see them or they are graduating," he blurted out with emotion.

EDUCABLE MOMENT HERE . . . Here's the feeling of the experience I talk about in my child that leads to his thoughts of a dog that leads to his decision to buy a dog.

Parenting to the feeling of the experience allows me to know why my son chooses what he chooses and more importantly, allows Justin to understand why he chooses what he chooses. Now, that's being "comfortable in his own skin."

Did I want Justin to buy a dog right now? No. Did I have a hundred reasons why he shouldn't do that right now? Of course. Was Justin going to be defensive and fight me on every judgment I have? Absolutely! Was Justin going to get this dog, with or without my blessing? You betcha!

Justin feels SAFE bringing his feelings forward in our relationship. Believe me . . . he does it quite often. Parenting to his feelings isn't always easy for me because I do want to protect him from some of his choices. But I can't by judging him through my fears.

I can, though, be the "safe place" for him to process the intention of the feelings of his own experience. I truly believe that raising Justin to be honest about his feelings, safe to share them openly with me, and learn from the process of what HE is experiencing, is CRUCIAL to his identity, his voice and his self-esteem. It also teaches him to be confident in his decision making without fear of failure.

Raising Justin to be a confident, self-regulated adult is certainly more important than MY opinion about his choice to get a dog.

By the way, when you have the safety between a child and a parent as I have with Justin, you can help them strategize about a plan of action based on the choices being made.

Bottom line: Justin is buying himself a dog. He heard my coaching and advising about options that fit his circumstance. He made his decision to get his puppy his way after considering the various plans we discussed. His feelings of loneliness were shared safely and they were validated by his parent. The facts about the expenses and timing were discussed. A strategy including the facts while honoring the intention of the feelings created decisions and a plan of action. Justin chose a plan of action that I would not have chosen. But it isn't me, it's him . . . and he has to live with the decisions he makes, as all of us do.

My job, as his parent, was to be a safe place for him to process the intention of his feelings, and guide him to all the facts of his circumstance, so that he can make an educated decision.

Linda and I have welcomed our new "grandpuppy" Rory, a pure white German Shepard to our family. More importantly, we have welcomed our son to a safe place to be himself . . . ALWAYS RESPOND, NEVER REACT.

Many of you are just starting out as parents or have younger children. What effect does "reaction" have on the little ones? Why is "responsive parenting" so important for little children?

Young children are constantly developing by trying out their decisions as it relates to the rules their parents set for them. Not unlike teenagers, young children get redirected to their parents' reaction from their own feelings when parents emote, react and judge their behavior.

A parent's reaction may get the desired outcome from their young child.

The child may be scared into compliance by the emotion of the parent. Goal accomplished, right? Well, not exactly. Young children become so afraid of their parents' reaction, that they cease to feel their own experience, and their identity now gets wrapped up in keeping their parent pleased. Young children, ultimately, want to please their parents. Their effort, intention to try and decision making are no longer characteristics of their self-esteem. Their self-esteem is not connected to their effort to try, and their own decision making process. Their identity and self-esteem is connected solely to their parents' approval of them.

Dangerous! Why? Because a child will learn to comply to get approval rather than self-regulate from the own feelings, thoughts, decisions and actions. Young children find themselves living in the judgment from the most important people in their lives. Parents will cease to be a safe place over time and the fear of disapproval becomes the prevailing feeling the child has in the moment of their experience.

Here's another Justin story. But this time, it relates back to when he was a young boy . . . Like many of you, I was taught to parent with judgment and reaction. I wasn't always as skilled at Responsive Parenting as I feel that I am today.

When my children were very young, I reacted a great deal to their decisions and behavior. I wasn't one of those parents who cared whether they were behaving comparatively to other kids, but I certainly held a standard up for them and judged them to that standard.

As a young therapist working with so many families, I began to question what we were doing to our children with reaction and judgment. I began to develop my new perspective and model of a healthier approach to how parents "parent" their children.

The birth of Responsive Parenting as a model in my practice became the birth of a new me as a father. After all, I practice what I preach.

It was Christmas time, 1994. Justin was 4-years-old. Justin drove me crazy when he was a little boy and Christmas was a time when he was in full gear and out of control. "He's just a little boy," my mom used to say, justifying his behavior.

He made choices and behaved in a way that would constantly get a reaction out of me. (I was parenting as my father modeled before me. My father was a "yeller" when I was young. He reacted to everything my brother and I did. And, of course it always seemed that I did way more than my brother!) After awhile, it wasn't clear anymore what his true intention might be and what may have been manipulation to see what my reaction would be. When you are stuck in that paradigm, your young child's identity is wrapped up in your reaction. Remember?

One day, Justin and I were running a holiday errand at the Galleria Mall. We were going into the toy store to purchase his cousin, Sammi her Christmas present. I had made a promise to myself . . . no matter what we went through there, I was going to use this moment to begin breaking the old paradigm, and I was no longer going to react to Justin with emotion or judgment. Rather I was going to **respond** to what was going on in front of me, calmly and thoughtfully.

We parked the car in the adjacent parking garage to the mall. (By the way, I couldn't believe how lucky we were to find a parking space so quickly and so close! After all, it was right before Christmas!) I sat quietly and turned around to unbuckle my son from his seatbelt. (Remember, he was 4-years-old.) I looked at Justin and asked calmly what he was planning to do in the toy store. He looked at me puzzled and answered what he knew I wanted to hear . . . "Go get Sammi her Christmas gift," he mumbled. Perfect, right? No, hold on. Remember, compliance is not enough. I needed to know his intention of what he was going to do.

"Great Jus, that's great. What will you do when we walk into the store?" I calmly continued.

"What do you want me to do, Daddy"? He asked very confused.

You see, we never set up his expectations ahead of time where he was a part of the conversation. It was always my voice, not his in the process.

"Let's think about walking into the store. You love that store. It has all your favorite toys." I explained

"It sure does, Daddy! It has the cars I love and I bet it has the new Transformers and everything!"

"You sound so excited, Justin. But, how are you going to feel when we go into the store and only buy something for Sammi?" I went on, not waiting for him to talk.

The expression on Justin's face was one of pure horror and he began to cry.

You see, I would have set that little boy up for a power struggle had I not engaged him in a conversation about the intentions of his feelings. He is 4-years-old, for God's sake. He is walking into a toy store and I am going to expect him to pull it together himself or hear me react?

I waited as long as necessary until Justin calmed himself down. And that's when the "negotiating" began.

"Daddy, can I get just a little Matchbox car and I promise I won't ask for anything else?" he asked proudly.

"I am sorry Justin. We are going to hold hands, walk into the store and buy the doll for Sammi. We are not going to buy you anything today," I said firmly, all the while wondering if I'm being too firm.

"Okay Dad, if I have to," He resigned as if he just lost a boxing match to Mohammad Ali. Justin held my hand firmly as we walked into the mall and into the toy store.

The mall was mobbed and the toy store was overflowing. Kids were running amok everywhere. Some parents were yelling at their children. Some parents were renegotiating with their child to regain order. And some parents were oblivious to where their children were in the store as they waited in the long line to check out.

Justin let go of his grip on my hand, ran directly to the Matchbox cars, found a really cool red one and ran back to me pleading for his life. (Toy stores know exactly what they are doing. I swear they keep their Matchbox car display in the front of the store, just to torment parents like me.)

Okay, here was my moment of truth as a parent. I was NOT going to react as I would have before. I was going to respond to his feelings and hold him to his commitment to me to only get Sammi her gift. I quietly took the car from Justin, placed it back where it belonged, walked out of the store, and sat down on the ground right outside the store. (Yep, you read that correctly, I sat down on the floor to the side of the entrance of the store, right in the open area of the mall. I knew I had to take this noisy, chaotic, overly stimulating environment out of the equation.)

"Dad, what are you doing? What's wrong? I'm sorry, please stand up!" Justin cried. I held Justin on my lap, and whispered into his ear. "I'm sorry Jus. I didn't realize how hard this would be for you. Why don't we leave and I will come back again without you later. It's okay. You love Matchbox cars and it's hard to see them and not buy them."

Justin's stiffened body relaxed in my arms. He looked at me and hugged me tightly. You see, we forget that all children, even little ones have their own feelings, thoughts, and experiences. We just expect them to perform as we want them to because we have things to get accomplished and they are along for the ride.

Well, they do see the world through their own eyes and if we can thoughtfully respond to them and communicate with them about their experience, they may not feel condemned by us. They may even feel empowered.

"Daddy, can I get one car?" he tried one last time. "No, sweetie." I calmly said.

"Can I look while you buy Sammi"s gift?" he tried . . . once more with feeling.

"No, I need you to stand by me. It's just too crowded. Maybe another time," I said, hanging with him as long as he needed. Pause, deep sigh and . . . "Okay Daddy," he concluded.

Justin and I walked back into the toy store, holding hands. We walked right past the Matchbox cars without a word. (I swear his head turned 360 degrees, fixated on that little red car.) We found the doll Sammi wanted, waited in line, purchased the gift, and left the store.

Justin walked proudly to the car. You could tell by the bounce in his step. His internal voice regulated his behavior and he honored his commitment.

I, too, walked with a bounce in my step, feeling damn proud of my new-found parenthood and proud that I could respond to my child without reacting out of my own agenda.

Neither one of us brought the incident up again. This is a very important point. If I had gone on and on about how good he was or lectured him as to what he did wrong initially, we would fall right back into the paradigm of doing all this for me. The positive affirmation for Justin was actualized through my intention to honor his feelings and my responsive approach to his experience without changing the rules.

Justin felt empowered by his feelings being attended to responsively, without judgment, and the feelings he experienced while following through with his commitment to me. So, let's be clear here what lessons we learned from this story . . .

1. As a parent, I made a decision and a commitment to stop reacting, emoting and judging my son's behavior.
2. I stopped reacting and began responding to the feelings of his intention; what was his experience and why was he feeling what he was feeling.
3. I was going to coach, teach and guide my son through his experience, not mine.
4. I set the rules or guidelines upfront to what was expected for our experience at the toy store. (Clinically, we call this, "PRESCRIBING THE SYMPTOM" where we set up ahead of time, what is expected, what might happen and how to handle it.) To keep order in any experience, there is always a set of guidelines, rules or laws that govern all of us.
5. Justin and I made an attempt at accomplishing our commitment.

When he couldn't handle it, I stayed with his experience and didn't make it mine.

6. I removed us from the moment, calmed things down, and loved him through it by honoring his feelings.

7. I remained in authority by holding us to the rules we committed to originally while letting him decide if he could hold to them and try again.

8. I delivered myself throughout the experience with "loving neutrality."

DELIVERY IS EVERYTHING HERE!

Deliver yourself thoughtfully, with respect for your child's position, and with kindness in your voice, regardless of how afraid or frustrated you may feel.

Parents, you are there to partner with your child and coach them. You are NOT there to control their thinking and actions to comply with your preference.

I was busy that day in the mall, but never too busy to guide my child through a difficult experience for him. Guiding and teaching them is NOT demanding they be who you want them to be. Trust in yourself as your child's parent. Guiding, coaching and teaching them with skill building, information gathering and with the knowledge of your preference will be impactful. **You are the most influential person in your child's life for most of their growing up. Stay humble to that fact. TRUST in yourself that you will remain an authority, even IF you relinquish the power over them.**

Power struggles with your child yields no winner. The more the power struggle, the less authority you retain. Trust in your child.

We all have feelings of intention in the moment of our experience and from that we have thoughts that make decisions to take action. (Feeling. Thought. Decision. Action.)

Preserve the process with them and your child will feel confident in the voice of their own choices. After all, it is THEIR experience, NOT yours.

Just a quick side note here . . . When I first met Linda, the love of my life, she once said to me that maybe I was "too nice." She had never met someone who didn't yell *much,* (I am human, you know!) and that she wasn't all that comfortable with it at first.

I responded with my true belief that how we choose to deliver ourselves is our choice. I never understood how we could treat the people we cared for with anger, disrespect and negativity. But we allow for that in our world. I believe that my opinion or preference is NEVER more important than respecting the person right in front of me.

If a parent can learn to deliver themselves through a RESPONSE rather than a REACTION, they are going to establish a DIALOGUE with their child about "what is" the truth of their child's experience.

The child feels the safety of that dialogue and the confidence in themselves to have a voice in their partnership with their parents.

RESPONSIVE PARENTING requires you to step away from the old model of REACTING and THINK before you speak.

Response is the expression of thoughts about your feelings. Parents want to make sure that their intention is to have dialogue and strategize with their child, rather than control the child's experience to create a preferred outcome.

Respond to your child's experience rather than react to your own feelings of their decisions or behaviors. This, my fellow parents, is very difficult to do, until you do it. Then it's everything!

Here's another great little example of what we are talking about . . .

Leslie Cochran is a single mom of two boys, Matt, 16, and Jake, 14. Leslie is a professional woman who owns her own boutique consulting firm. This allows an adequate income and provides her plenty of time to be home with her boys.

She has been divorced from the boys' father, Doug, for 10 years. The boys have lived in this blended family longer than they ever lived in the original family unit.

Doug Cochran is remarried to Rebecca, who has three children of her own. Doug and Rebecca also have a 3-year-old daughter together. Matt and Jake live primarily with their mother and are supposed to "visit" their dad, Doug, at his home, every other weekend and one time during the week. (The truth is, though, that the boys don't always feel comfortable going.)

Leslie Cochran is a very dedicated parent and works hard to undo what she has learned as a reactive parent and become a more responsive mother to her boys. For years, the boys had three parents reacting to them, trying to fit them into a "picture" neither one of them could successfully achieve. In the socio-economic cultural world that this group strived to participate in, there was an expectation that boys have a certain look, attend certain schools and play certain sports. Somehow, once again, that "everybody else" group set standards that this parent group felt pressure to live up to.

It seemed like every week one or both of the boys were having "special meetings" with their parents about their performance in school, or their athletics. The boys were constantly reprimanded for their grades or lack of effort and new "plans" were negotiated to assist them to try harder and to perform better.

The difficulty through the years of this family's co-parenting is that Doug and Rebecca have completely bought into the model of living in these "pictures" with their children and expecting them to follow the agenda of "everybody else." Leslie, however, never really felt comfortable with this approach to parenting Matt and Jake.

The discussions with Matt and Jake were always filled with comparisons to Rebecca's three other children or comparisons with what the community expected. Neither boy had a true voice with their parents . . . *any* of their parents for that matter. Each boy quickly learned to say what their parents wanted to hear, just to get through the moment. Somehow, that seemed to satisfy their parents until the next time.

Ultimately, though, each boy went back to what they were choosing to do in the first place. The ongoing lack of integrity was being fostered in this dynamic. The boys learned to say one thing and then intended to do another. Not good. Not good at all.

This dynamic went around and around between the boys and their three parents . . . for years and years. As the boys grew and developed, they, each in their own way, became more and more defiant, angry, and vocal. (As I have said to you before . . . just because the child's feelings are forced to be redirected, doesn't mean they go away!)

Leslie's role with her boys was to desperately find a way to motivate the boys to perform so that the judgment from the "other side" (Doug and Rebecca) would stop. She thought, if they performed well, they would fit the picture and feel better about themselves. And if they fit the picture, the other parents would feel better about them too.

She tried, but with no success. She had to do something. It was time for Leslie to take a different approach.

(Do you remember in Chapter Four, I opened with a story about my daughter Elizabeth and Mrs. Schwartz asking her if she was ready to "compete?" I wrote then that as a parent, I couldn't change the culture of the school district, BUT, perhaps I could create a family culture at home that would balance the intensity and stress for Lizzy?)

Leslie Cochran had to stop trying to fit her boys into the agenda of others. She also had to stop trying to change the agenda of the others as well, namely Doug and Rebecca, by convincing them to approach their life or the boys differently.

Leslie needed to look at the family culture she was creating and the boys' experience in her own home. The family culture for she and her boys was really all she had control over, anyway.

She had to decide whether she could RESPOND to who they are, rather than REACT to who "they should be." She had to change her reactions to responses without judgment and promote a voice in Matt and Jake.

Matt and Jake felt awkward and confused. They couldn't understand why their mom wasn't yelling anymore and why the "special meetings" had stopped. Leslie learned to deliver herself differently . . . with calm and kindness . . . with preference, rather than judgment. There was no agenda in her home other than to promote and embrace the truth of who each boy was, at any given moment. So, here's what happened . . .

Jake came home after school one day, with a new Mohawk haircut. Jake is a great kid, but recently has been vocalizing anger about not being able to do what he wants and having to follow the rules adults have set up for him. He expressed "hating to go over to his father's house" and not wanting to try in school with the tutors that he works with.

His father and stepmother continued to call for a "special meeting" but Leslie and the boys were not participating in those anymore.

Back to the Mohawk . . . Leslie took one look at her son and REACTED! "What in the hell have you done to your beautiful hair? What is wrong with you, Jake?" she screeched at the top of her lungs.

Jake, getting from his mom what he expected, ran right up to his room, slammed the door and spent the night in his room there. Leslie took a seat in her living room and sat quietly wiping away her tears. She knew that her reaction took away her opportunity to parent her son. She didn't respond; she reacted. Something was obviously up with Jake but now Leslie's reaction became the focus of the moment.

It was no longer about Jake. It was now about Leslie's judgment (fear) about Jake and what Doug, Rebecca and "everybody else" would think about Jake's new look AND about her effectiveness as his mother. This was Leslie's moment of truth.

It was time to undo the model of judgment, once and for all and respond to her son's experience. He needed her, so it was time to parent differently.

Leslie knocked softly on Jake's door around 8:30 p.m. that night. She waited until he gave his permission to enter. That was a first as well. Normally she opened as she knocked, as many parents do.

She sat on the side of the bed, purposely looking at Jake's eyes, and ignoring the Mohawk itself. It just didn't really matter anymore.

"What . . . what? You hate it, don't you? Well I love it and I'm not cutting it off!" Jake proclaimed with determination and courage.

"I love you Jake." whispered Leslie. "I love you any way you are and any way you want to be," she said in tears.

"I just wanted to do what I want to do, Mom. I'm so tired being told what to do and being yelled at by everybody!" Jake said as he sobbed into his mother's arms.

You see, it took everything in Leslie's power not to dive into a familiar speech of . . . "But Jake, if you only tried harder and followed the plan, life would be so much easier!" (The last thing Jake needed in this moment was to be judged. He was raw, sharing his experience, his frustration and his pain.)

Instead, Leslie partnered with Jake and they strategized how it could be different in their home, their family culture, so that he could feel empowered to have a voice in his life, while still living within Leslie's values, morals and basic rules. Her values, morals and basic rules are specific to her world view, not an agenda to fit into anyone else's picture.

Leslie and Jake both fell asleep on Jake's bed and when Leslie awoke at three in the morning to go back into her own bedroom, she gazed at her little boy sleeping there with the goofiest hairdo one could imagine resting on the pillow. And this was what she was so afraid of? A Mohawk?

Leslie never brought up the hairdo again. Two weeks later, Jake came home with his head shaved, and the Mohawk was history.

She didn't react at all this time, but gave a thoughtful response . . . inquiring about his choice to cut it off. "Jake, you decided to cut off your Mohawk?" she inquired innocently and without reaction. (Although inside she wanted to dance the Cha Cha!)

"Yeah . . . it's no big deal," Jake said as he munched on a homemade brownie.

Leslie later learned from Matt, Jake's older brother, that Jake had asked the prettiest girl in his class to "go out" and that she explained to Jake that she would have said yes, had he left his beautiful hair alone. She could not "date" a guy with a Mohawk.

Parents live in fear of their children's voice. They don't trust that their child will "figure it out" in time and learn from the experience of the process of their own life. Parents often feel embarrassed by their children's decisions because they are so fearful of "everybody else's" judgment.

Children are NOT an extension of their parents. They are their own person with their own ideas and their own feelings.

Do we really believe that the influence of a parent's modeling of their own preference has no effect on their child's experience? Of course it must . . . it is the most significant "frame of reference" children have for most of their growing up.

Responding to what our children choose allows us to thoughtfully guide and coach them, without controlling their experience or their outcome.

Reacting to our children out of our own feelings changes the focus from their experience to ours. It pushes away the feelings of their experience and redirects their attention to our reactions, our feelings, and our unsolicited expression of our preference (judgment).

These "pushed away" feelings don't go away, they just build up inside. At some point these feelings re-emerge and must be attended to one way or another.

Jake spent his life frustrated about the expectations, control and judgment his parents had and their lack of receptiveness to hearing his voice. His feelings were spilling out all over the place.

Do we really think he didn't know how his mother would feel about his choice of hairdo? Did "Mohawk Jake" really think he would be welcome with open arms by his parents? Of course not. Jake had to express himself in such a way to create the conflict he was used to. His choice elicited a reaction out of Leslie that he manipulated to validate that choice. He was more focused on his mother's reaction that he didn't have to feel the truth of his intention. His intention was to get a reaction out of his mother and out of "everybody else." It had nothing to do with his haircut.

The truth, without judgment of Jake, allows Leslie to understand the intention of the feelings of her son's choice. As she responds to her son's voice, she helps Jake stay in the intention of his feelings about his own experience, rather than making HER the focus of his intention.

Leslie guided Jake to "OWN" his own life experiences. She stepped away from reacting to her own judgment of him and began listening and responding to the voice of his experience.

Jake's mother is now appropriately a safe place for him. She is back on the "sidelines" of Jake's experience . . . ready to coach, teach, and guide him, delivering with "loving neutrality."

Now, that's healthy parenting!

CHAPTER SIX

Family Culture

Family culture is a dynamic, living, breathing experience that protects, nurtures and identifies the lives of those individuals who belong to it.

I remember many wonderful memories of my childhood; some not quite so wonderful, and many indelible images I have never forgotten that identify me to the family culture I come from.

I remember the wonderful aroma of homemade sweet and sour meatballs filling our home every year on the Rosh Hashanah (Jewish New Year) holiday. Linda tries to replicate my mother's secret recipe for me on special occasions. (Now that's true love!)

I remember each member of my family sitting at the kitchen table, in the same seat, for every meal we ate at home. The table was rectangular with my dad at the head by the window; my mom at the other end by the wall phone, and my brother and I on each side between our parents; him on the left, me on the right. It was unspoken, but each of us considered the seat we sat in to be our very own.

I remember lying in my bed, listening to my parents arguing with one another about my father's "yelling" and feeling extremely protective of my mom as my father yelled at her.

I remember the rule we had about not being allowed to have a pet in our apartment. My parents were landlords, since they always owned the buildings we lived in, and they made a rule that there were no pets allowed in the building.

If they allowed us, they would have to let the tenants have pets too. So, no pets growing up.

SIDE NOTE . . . Confession time. Big sigh.

When I was 11-years-old, my friend Marty and I went on a bus across town to the local pet store. Try letting your 11-year-old do that in today's world! You see, I was about to go "underground" with my friend Marty. I was sick and tired of how "mean" my dad was being about this no pet rule. We were not allowed to even discuss the topic.

So I took this thing into my own hands. Every Saturday morning the pet store we often traveled to on the bus offered free kitten adoptions to families. Marty and I walked into the store one Saturday morning, and I walked right up to the lady sitting behind the table and boldly asked for my kitten. She smiled and handed me a parental consent form and explained that I needed my parent's signature to pick my kitty. I looked boldly into her eyes and lied through my teeth! (Gasp . . . come on now, I was eleven-years-old. The kitty I had my eye on was a Tabby and I loved Tabbies.)

I told her my mother was waiting outside in the car and I would be right back. (By the way, my mother didn't even drive a car back then.) I returned with a forged signature with my mothers name scribbled on the appropriate line. I took my kitten and walked out of the store, scared to death. I know I was young, but WHAT THE HELL WAS I THINKING? What was I going to do now? The only thing I could do . . . sneak the Tabby into my bedroom and live like a fugitive.

Once my parents found out and the yelling subsided, I spent the next three days walking door to door throughout all the neighborhoods around us to find the cat a home. There was no discussion, no mercy. On the third day, a nice older lady living alone, took pity on me, and took my kitty as her own. Back to my childhood memories . . .

I remember the sounds of the many languages my father spoke; English, Yiddish, Polish, and Russian, filling the kitchen on any given evening with accents as thick as the sauce on my mother's infamous meatballs.

My father, Joe Dembo, was always on the phone talking to someone about business. He was a Holocaust survivor and used his survival instincts everyday of his life. Thinking back, it's really was quite amazing. All the Survivors I knew were multilingual. Why? In order to survive.

I remember late nights when I was a little boy, lying on the floor next to my mother's side of the bed, talking to her in the dark while my father snored away. (I was always in physical pain with my scoliosis and lying on the ground helped. My mom was always willing to keep me company.) **These memories are the experiences of my FAMILY'S CULTURE.**

Family culture is the physical and emotional environment of the total experience of our identity growing up as a family member.

Family Culture is the "incubator of identity" both for the individual and the collective whole.

FAMILY CULTURE is that place that must hold safely, the child's experience growing up. As all culture, it is the interplay of the "FOUR R's" . . . RULES, ROLES, RITUALS, and RELATIONSHIPS.

As a dynamic place for experience and identity to cultivate, the Family Culture embraces the exchange between Rules, Roles, Rituals and Relationships.

RULES . . . The Family Culture, like all culture, is structurally and interactionally designed to safely develop the identity of each member while holding to a set of boundaries constructed to keep ORDER and STABILITY. PARENTS are responsible for the family culture they create for themselves and their children. They have the AUTHORITY to choose the values, morals, and ethics they wish to model in their home and thus, create the rules necessary to uphold their beliefs.

Parents build the structure of the daily experience a child has, as they grow up in their family home. Children DO NOT CHOOSE where they live, what to eat and how their meals are prepared; whether religion is a part of their daily life or what activities and responsibilities will be expected of them. Children have no authority or voice unless it is developed and promoted in the culture by the parents. Parents make all those RULES until such a time in a child's development when they are ready to live by their own set of rules.

Each one of us lives as a citizen in our local communities, and as a part of larger national community. As local citizens of our neighborhoods and municipalities, we understand and operate by the laws (rules) and expectations specific to being a "good citizen" in that community. As citizens of our national community, we, too, understand the laws and expectations specific to being "good citizens" in this larger culture. We are given the FREEDOM TO CHOOSE how we will embrace and participate as individual citizens in the culture we live in, given our understanding of the laws that govern us. We are expected to self-regulate, to self-govern, within the culture, given our individual experience in our larger community.

FAMILY CULTURES are no different than the larger communities we live in.

Parents are the GOVERNING BODY of the "family community; the family culture" they have created. Children are "citizens" in this family community. They must learn to live respectfully and effectively in the culture they grow up in. They, however, like all citizens, MUST be given the freedom to choose how they will approach, embrace and participate as INDIVIDUAL citizens in the culture of their family. They must be given the freedom to be "empowered" to feel the moment of their experience within the family culture they reside. If not, children like citizens of all cultures will find a way to revolt or create an underground lifestyle, out of the view of their governing body.

For parents, the process of communicating the rules, expectations, and standards in a family community REQUIRES the same consistent structure and leadership as the elected officials of our larger communities are charged with accomplishing.

All cultures require leadership, structure and a process of communication to keep ORDER, while promoting each individual citizen to self-regulate and NAVIGATE themselves throughout the culture.

As leaders of the family culture, parents must be clear to its citizens about what the set of rules are and what the consequences are for rules broken. In the larger society, we live by a "constitution" that embodies all the rules and regulations necessary to keep order. It is each citizen's responsibility to have a working knowledge of this constitution as a way to live peacefully.

One premise remains a foundation for all cultures . . . **Every citizen has a right to live their life individually and peacefully within the rules that govern them.** Each citizen has a right to their own voice, their own identity and their own experience.

ROLES . . . In every culture, each citizen has a role to play in the dynamic of the culture as a whole. Each member contributes to the functioning of the family system as a living, breathing individual and as a part of the total entity. In families the roles played by each member depends first and foremost on the vision the parents have for their family. Children growing up in a family must feel the importance of their role. Each family member, including every aged child, brings to the culture a unique set of qualities that add to the complexion and identity of the family.

Parents must recognize that children are participating members and that their roles must give them a voice in the process of the family culture. Children must be given clear boundaries to the role they play while feeling the affirmation and validation necessary to build a strong sense of self from the importance of that role. Parents need to remain cognizant of these factors as they develop their standards, expectations, ethics and values of the family they are leading.

The roles in a family are changing today as the complexion and structure of the family changes in society as a whole. The frequency and prevalence of divorce has forever changed the identity of families in today's world. The roles of both parents and kids in the family system must be viewed differently as the needs of the family are adapting to the change of the family as we know it.

The pressures of the economy, and the changes in the role of a "stay at home parent" from a necessity to a luxury, has also forever changed the roles (and relationships) of all members of the family unit.

The ability to become a parent through science or through the adoption process as a single person or same sex couple has also changed the face of the family and thus the roles in the family.

The family that Dr. Spock spoke about in the 1950's and the family we speak about today are very different animals. Roles and responsibilities in the family that may have been seen one way in the "classic" family structure are now being looked at differently in the "modern" family structure.

We now have many faces to the appearance of a family in society and many views to the roles of its members. However, one thing remains true in any family . . . all family members have a role in the functioning and identity of the family unit.

Family roles, like the families themselves, must remain flexible and malleable to the circumstances facing the specific family culture at any given time in its development. Roles in the family include functional roles and relational roles.

For example . . . A child's responsibility for their chores is as important to their identity development as a parent's identity as an income producer.

A child's role as rational thinker amongst their siblings is as important a role as one parent's role as the "organized one" in the daily coordination with the other parent.

The roles we take on and the response we receive for our approach to these roles is critical to the functioning AND the identity of the individual and the family.

A strong family identity comes from a strong sense of its role as a family unit.

And a strong individual identity comes from a strong sense of the individual's role in that family unit.

RITUALS . . . As a family culture operates within its rules and its roles, it is the CONSISTENCY of the experience that helps form these experiences into the IDENTITY of the family. The rules and roles need to remain malleable to the circumstances that may face the family system. BUT all cultures need order and each citizen needs to know that they can trust that order for self-regulation.

RITUALS help create identity because the consistent nature of a ritual, chosen by the parents, honored by the family, identifies the priorities of its members. Rituals allow all members to organize their lives around experiences they can count on. It creates that safety and calm parents attempt to create, as a predictable experience for themselves and their children.

Think about the memories you have of your own childhood and about the rituals your family prioritized while you were growing up. Why do these rituals come to our memory so easily? Because they were constant, consistent and repetitious and created meaning to our experience. We can count on them. **Rituals define our family experience.**

Do you remember as we opened this chapter I shared with you my memories about my mom's sweet and sour meatballs? Well, just the smell of those meatballs will bring back an entire holiday experience for me. We honored the holiday of Rosh Hashanah the same way every year of my childhood, just like millions of Jewish families did and still do today.

The actual synagogue service and those rituals have been around throughout history and millions of people follow the ritual of those services each and every year. The magnitude of that holiday is the deep connection to the fact that people throughout history performed the very same rituals.

But for me, it was my parents' preference to create the family meal they chose and the "meatball ritual" that defined the experience of the holiday and actually for all those who attended each year.

I can remember my cousin asking as he walked into my parents' house for the holiday dinner every year, "Hey Aunt Goldie, did you make your special meatballs this year?" He always received the same answer. (Yes, that's right . . . my mother's actual first name was Goldie. In fact her maiden name was Goldie Diamond. Great name, isn't it?)

Parents create rituals based on their own preference and priorities. For the child, these rituals contribute to the intention of the feeling of their experience and the identity they create around these experiences.

Children grow up in the sounds, smells, tastes and feel of each ritual of their family experience. As their identity, rituals become THEIR family history . . . which identifies and differentiates their experience from any other family's.

(More on rituals in the next chapter.)

RELATIONSHIPS . . . The last of the Four R's is the relationships in the family that bring together the quality of the experience in the family culture.

You can have a solid structure of rules, defined roles and rituals that support the identity development of each member, but without healthy communication between the members, the quality of the moment is compromised.

This all starts with the standard by which the parents decide to communicate with one another . . . their relationship. Even in single parent families and "only" parent families, the tone for the relationships in the family unit is set by the way the parent operates in their own relationships.

"Rules of engagement" is that standard parents must set for communicating through conflict and pain, as well as through joy and pleasure. How parents deliver themselves, will model for their children the communication dynamic permissible for all members to engage in. If you communicate through anger or judgment, the culture will give way to anger and judgment. If you communicate through nurturance and respect, the culture will give way to nurturance and respect. Parents set the relationship model and children grow up in what their parents have created.

Feeling. Thought. Decision. Action . . . If parents prioritize communication in their family culture that honors "feelings" as well as thoughts, decisions and actions, the relationship dynamics will thrive in "truth without judgment."

If parents communicate to the thoughts and decisions with little regard for feelings, they force the child to detach from their own feelings in order to communicate in the model established by their parents.

If parents create a dynamic in their family where children can have a voice and express their feelings of intention of the experience they are living in, the relationship they have with the other members feels safe and honest.

If children feel safe to have a voice in the family culture they are growing up in, their individual growth will feel safe and honest as well. Let me introduce you to the Siegels . . . .

Joanne and Tyler Siegel have three children. Rose, 16-years-old, is a sophomore at a very prestigious high school. Jeffrey, 18-years-old, is a freshman at a private college on the East Coast. And Annie, 21-years-old, is a senior at a very large university in the Midwest.

Tyler Siegel is a very successful business man in the community and Joanne is very active in philanthropy. The Siegel family is a very close family with a very strong identity, both as individual members and collectively as a group. This is exactly the way Tyler and Joanne intended it to be.

You see, the Siegels understand Family Culture and their role as parents within the culture they have developed.

Tyler and Joanne were married 25 years ago. They consciously and purposely set out back then to create the family culture they were comfortable living in, for them and their future children.

They modeled specifically the values and standards they believe in and have guided their children accordingly. The Siegels value religion and created very specific associations and rituals throughout the years. They value family togetherness and have structured seasonal trips, weekend activities, rituals with extended family members, and daily family dinners to give their children the milieu necessary to experience the identity of the "Tyler and Joanne Family."

The Siegels value education and placed each of the three children in the schools they believed would prepare them best for the next step in their educational journey. Each child attended the most prestigious private elementary and secondary private schools in the area.

All of these values are extremely strong for the Siegels and have become a very important part of their identity. Communicating with respect, living with integrity, and the pursuit of knowledge are so fundamental to the Siegels that any deviation from these values feels crisis-like to all of them.

Growing up in the Siegel house was easy in many ways. The parents did a wonderful job being consistent with who they are and communicating that to their children throughout their children's experience growing up. The standards are high, everyone knows it and everyone buys into it.

The Siegel family structure is so consistent and so clear that all a child needs to do is embrace the culture and put forth their own individual efforts.

Rose, Jeffrey, and Annie, each found their unique and individual way to experience the family culture their parents created. They exercised their individual choices based on the intentions of their feelings of the culture their parents had set up for all of them to live in. The Siegels figured it out and understood the power and influence of the family culture in the development of their children. They are awesome parents with equally awesome kids!

Rose Siegel is the youngest child and the last to attend the prestigious private high school. In two and a half more years, Tyler and Joanne will be "empty-nesters." It will be a sad time for the Siegels since the experience they created for their family felt so magical.

Rose has always been a vocal child about her likes, her dislikes, and her preferences. She was the most vocal and "toughest" child for the Siegels to communicate with. It seemed as if Rose challenged her parents on everything.

The Siegels felt that the culture allowed for Rose's voice as it did for everyone else. She just exercised it more frequently. Rose never really took it so far, though, that she would be defiant or out of control. She was just always "pushing" her parents to explain "why" they were making the decisions, they were making. Rose was all about "intention."

At the beginning of her sophomore year of high school, when both her siblings were now out of the house and away at college, Rose completely shut down.

(Remember, Rose was the vocal one but never really acted out in a way that was problematic. Her parents were always concerned about her attitude, but she complied with the standards of her culture.)

"Rose, what is going on with you?" her mom asked.

"Nothing, please just leave me alone," Rose answered flatly. (I told you she complied even when she was upset. She said "please" while pushing her mom back a bit.)

"Rose, you matter so much to me and I am here if you need me." Mom said, attempting to create a safe place for Rose's feelings.

A few days went by and nothing seemed to improve in Rose's mood. Joanne was overwhelmed with concern but didn't know what to do.

The family culture was in place. Their children had been doing so well and embracing everything the family identity stood for. Each child was successful in their own right, yet different from one another. The Siegels were proud of what they had created within their family.

What could possibly be wrong here that Rose wouldn't/couldn't reach out to her parents? Surely they were safe enough to help guide her through this?

I met with the Siegels in my office early one morning. They had heard about me from their friends and I certainly knew of the Siegel Family, as their name, was displayed on some huge building I pass on the way to my office everyday. They told me the story of Rose and wanted me to see her.

"She must be depressed. There must be something going on with a boy!" Tyler began, listing off possibilities.

"Woa, slow down Mr. Siegel. We have no idea what Rose is feeling," I stopped him from hypothetically speaking for Rose's experience and began to ask about the dynamics in the family culture.

It was clear to me that these were not parents who were angry, attacking and judgmental of their child. They were genuinely concerned, caring and delivering themselves very appropriately. It was in their history of their family dynamics that they could find the clues about Rose.

Rose was the youngest and her role was changing. She was now an "only child" at home in this family of high standards. She was no longer camouflaged by her brother and sister and THEIR approach to the family. Rose could no longer "swim in the wake" of her siblings' "stroke." (Swimming metaphor . . . When you swim in someone else's wake, you can coast behind their lead.)

In the Siegels' effort to create this amazing family culture, perhaps they didn't provide flexibility for individual ideas or experience? Maybe the Siegels' relationship with Rose wasn't what they thought it was? Maybe Rose had feelings about the new dynamics with her parents without her siblings at home?

Okay, I know what you are asking yourself, "What's he saying now?" I thought he said that the family dynamics the Siegels created in their family culture allowed for the child's individual thought? They did allow for individual thought and expression BUT perhaps only about the standards, decisions, and choices Tyler and Joanne held to be important. Maybe it wasn't safe to truly challenge their thinking?

Rose shut down when her last sibling, Jeffrey left for school, which coincided with the beginning of her sophomore year of high school. The Siegels expected life to continue as before, just without Jeffrey at home. Why not? When Annie left for school, Jeffrey and Rose didn't miss a beat.

I recommended that the Siegels go home and at dinner, bring up the observation that perhaps since Jeffrey left for college, Rose may be uncomfortable. (I knew it was important here that Rose doesn't feel as if something is wrong with her for having her feelings, so I wasn't about to recommend that she come in for therapy. It wasn't necessary yet, if ever.

Joanne began the conversation about Jeffrey leaving for college and how different it must feel for Rose. Rose perked right up and looked cautiously at her parents.

"What's going on? What do you mean?" she boldly asked.
"I don't know, maybe you are sad about Jeffrey leaving or being alone without him?" Dad answered cautiously himself. Rose began to chuckle . . .

"You think I miss Jeffrey? Don't get me wrong, of course I do . . . a little. No, I am upset because without Jeffrey here, I'm left for you to focus all your attention on me and expect me to do things. I hate what you make me do and I hate the school you make me go to!" she yelled.

(If there was a time for that suspenseful "Rocky" music that plays every time Rocky starts to change the fight against Apollo Creed, this would be the moment for Rose!)

Tyler and Joanne were floored, stunned and silent. They could not believe what they just heard. You see, the family culture had it all, with all the best intentions and great skill by these two wonderful parents. They just never thought that their children would question their structure, their values or their choices and not feel able to bring it to them for discussion.

"Why didn't you ever tell us you felt that way?" Joanne sadly questioned.

"Are you kidding me? I challenge everything you say. I just never think you take me seriously so I do what I'm supposed to do." Rose explained bravely.

"I hate my school, didn't you know that?"

"We thought you struggled there but we never thought you hated it. It's where your sister and brother went and graduated from. We want all three of you to finish there and go onto great colleges."

"I know, that's why I didn't say anything. It's not up to me. I don't ever have a say in my life. God, I cannot wait 'til I grow up!" Rose said as she began to tear up. (Yes, a bit dramatic, but she is only 16-years-old.)

The Siegels were speechless and finished dinner quickly. They were truly at a loss for words. After all, they were not going to abandon the strong family culture they worked so hard to create.

In my office, Joanne finished telling me the story of their dinner as she broke down in tears.

"Does she hate us?"

"No, if she hated you, she would never have tried to comply with your rules, and expectations. Think about how it might feel to live in your parents' family culture, and not feel you fit into it like your siblings do. You see, we parent to the intention of the feelings of each child's experience.

"What is Rose's experience?" I inquired.

"What should we do?" asked Joanne.

"Ask Rose and listen to her feelings," I said and I walked her to the door.

Rose began to cry as her parents asked her how she felt and what she would like for them to change for her.

"I waited for this day my whole life. Really, you want to know what I want? Okay, here goes . . . I want to change schools and go to the public school where Ashley and Emily go." she said firmly, hyperventilating. (Ashley and Emily are friends with Rose from religious school and the three of them hang out all the time.)

Silence filled the room for several minutes before Rose said, "You see, I told you, you wouldn't let me do what I want. You want me to stay where I am now because that's where you want all of us to graduate from. Let's not put ourselves through this, okay?" Rose demanded as she got up and left the room.

She was right and the Siegels knew it. Joanne and Tyler talked for hours about Rose's desire to change schools. Should they hold the line to their values here and just get her through the next two years? Should they let her go be with her friends at the public school? What will college officials think about two high schools showing up on her transcript? Maybe it will look like she couldn't handle it at the private school?

The Siegels were reeling in fear and unable to wrap their heads around Rose's feelings because they were reacting to their own. Parents need the courage to RESPOND to their children's feelings, while honoring their own.

The Siegels and I met for a strategy session. They walked in as if someone had died, as I proceeded to share my excitement at the opportunity they had here with their wonderful daughter, Rose. (Attitude is everything when attempting to respond rather than react!)

"Tyler, Joanne . . . you are very good parents and have created an amazing family for Rose, Jeffrey and Annie. You are so fortunate that you have this opportunity to guide and teach Rose about her feelings. Rose just needs to be heard. She needs to know you take her feelings seriously, no matter what decision is made. I am not telling you to let her change schools. I am telling you to show her you are willing to integrate her feelings into your preference and see where they fit."

"In English please," Tyler said with a smile.

"Become educated consumers on her behalf. Have you met with the other school? Have you talked to the headmaster of the school she is currently attending? Have you let her know you are willing to thoughtfully consider her feelings before sticking with your original choice? Perhaps what Rose really needs to know is that no matter what, she is more important to you than the picture you have for her."

"Oh, I get it. Show her we are willing to explore her idea," Tyler reacted.

"No, not exactly! Don't do any of this disingenuously. You would have to agree between yourselves that you are truly willing to explore all of this for her and stay true to the process of Rose's feelings. This cannot be a manipulation to placate Rose."

"So . . . go meet with her school and let them know how she is feeling. Go meet with the other school and see if we are comfortable if she were to transfer. And let Rose know we are willing to do all that before we categorically say no to her idea." Joanne put together.

"Absolutely . . . awesome parenting! Rose may never move schools, but she at least will learn she doesn't have to keep her feelings from you because you will respond to her seriously and with respect," I said proudly. (I just love it when parents "get it!")

Tyler had to leave town for business after our meeting, so the Siegels decided rather than wait for his return, Joanne would talk to Rose that very night.

"Rose, let me tell you what your dad and I decided to do. We love you and we don't want you to withhold your feelings in fear of us not taking you seriously. I am sick knowing you feel like we never hear you. I am sorry."

"Please Mom; can't we just let this alone?"

"Please Rose, listen! We have decided that I will go meet with both schools and learn what I can about the public school and if you can get the same level of classes there as you are getting where you are. I have a meeting and a tour this Thursday. I am also meeting tomorrow with Mr. Lewen at your school to find out his thoughts about you possibly leaving and if it hurts your chances in college." (Mr. Lewen is the college counselor at Roses school.)

"Wow, I don't know what to say. Thank you. But I never thought you would do any of this. Let's just leave it alone. I'm fine, really. I will be happier at home, promise."

"Rose, if this matters to you, it matters to us. I will tell you, I don't want you to leave your high school, but I think I'm being selfish. I'm not you. So let's get our information and then go from there." Her mom said as they both began to cry.

Rose and Joanne embraced. They went on with their week and didn't mention this again.

Joanne did her due diligence and reported back to Tyler who was still out of town. To Joanne's surprise, she found, for as much as she didn't want to, she could actually see Rose fitting into this new school much better than where she was currently attending.

She found the new school to be accommodating to Rose's academic plan and ready to embrace her with open arms. This actually caused more struggle in Joanne. It would have been much easier if the school just didn't impress her . . . but it did.

She found out from Mr. Lewen that he too felt comfortable with the move and since Rose had good grades, it would not be a problem with college admissions.

His one caution was that Rose could make this one move, BUT if she didn't like her new school, she really needed to remain there.

Joanne and Tyler needed to be on the same page here. Tyler was struggling with giving Rose a voice on something this important. Joanne was ready to give Rose permission to make her own choice.

As I have said before, these are good people who have created a great life for their children. The Siegels learned that they didn't fully communicate the openness they thought they had to ALL their children and now they needed the courage to change how their family culture responded to feelings beyond their own preferences.

Rose's parents brought a united front to their dinner meeting with Rose. "Okay, I met with the new school and with your current school." Joanne began.

"Well . . . what did everybody say? I'm staying, right?" Rose interrupted.

"No, actually, we were very impressed with the new school and Mr. Lewen said there would be no problem. He did say, if you made the move and didn't like it, you would have to stay and graduate from there." Joanne reported as Tyler sat quietly.

"So what does this mean?" Rose asked.

"It means that Mom and I feel that you are ready to make this decision and whatever you decide, we will support." Tyler said right on cue.

Rose sat with tears streaming down her cheeks. She didn't know what to say. Thank you seemed trite.

"I love you guys." Rose mustered.

In Rose's mind this moment was never going to come. But, ready or not, here it was and all her feelings of not being heard were now replaced with the stifling fear of making a life decision.

The Siegels were now in a position to guide and coach Rose in her decision based on her thoughts from her feelings.

Rose spent a day at the new school shadowing one of the students there. She met with the headmaster of the school she was currently attending. Rose was empowered to feel her own moment of her own experience. She did her own due diligence and was ready to make her decision.

At dinner one evening, Rose told her parents of her decision.

"If this is really my decision, then I have made a decision. I tried to keep an open mind about both schools and not just make a decision to prove a point. I know you guys want me to stay at my current school . . ."

"No, you do what you . . ."

"Please let me finish." Rose commanded.

Rose took a deep breathe and continued. "I know you guys want me to stay where I am, but I need to go where I'm comfortable. I would like to transfer to the new school for my junior year," Rose declared as if she just emancipated herself.

"We would like you to stay where you are, HOWEVER we know you need to leave and we support your choice. Rose, we don't have to agree with you to support your need to make this decision yourself. Your dad and I love you more than our need for you to do what we want you to do. We want to be there for you." Joanne said with joy for Rose and sadness for herself.

Rose Siegel lived within the rules of her family culture. She clearly embraced the role she played as the youngest of three high achieving kids with high achieving parents.

She loved the rituals her parents created for their family and identified herself by them. It was in the relationship dynamics and communication patterns where she found deep struggle with her parents. Rose had truly felt there was no resolution for her until she grew up and left home.

When her brother Jeffrey left for college, and there were no siblings left at home, she could no longer hide her feelings behind her compliance to the rules, roles and rituals.

She, finally had to confront the feelings left unattended, about her relationship with her parents and her belief that she had no permission to have her own voice. Rose found the courage to make her first true life decision and honor her true voice and represent her true identity. Tyler and Joanne Siegel found the courage to step aside and let her.

Family Culture is the "practice field" of life for our children. Parents supply everything that goes into the culture for our child's family experience . . . except the experience itself.

The child has their own experience of the moment and must feel empowered to make decisions based on the intention of their feelings with guidance from their parents.

The Family Culture, as an extension of the parent's preference, must be a safe place for the child to experience their growth and their own view of the world they live in.

The rules, roles, rituals and relationships that blend together to create the full experience of the culture, are essential to the parents view of their family identity.

They are equally essential to each individual member's view of themselves as it relates to the culture they live in.

CHAPTER SEVEN

Rules . . . To Live By

Family culture, like all culture, requires ORDER for its members to learn, grow and experience their life peacefully. Parents create their family culture with their own preferences, expectations, values, morals and ethics. To be effective in accomplishing a safe and orderly environment for their family members to live fully in the moment, parents must establish a set of RULES for the family culture itself.

RULES are the expectations and requirements that each individual must embrace, understand and follow for the culture to function effectively.

Remember from the last chapter . . . **Parents are the governing body for the family culture they create.**

Governments and their leaders from all cultures "govern" with a set of rules and a process by which these rules are enforced. An established set of boundaries known by all its citizens, allows each individual citizen to live within the guidelines, in their own way, without interference from the governing body, UNLESS, of course, the individual has stepped outside the boundaries of these guidelines and has broken one of the rules.

The premise here is that each individual citizen has the skills and tools available for them to navigate through the set of rules governing them and self-regulate in the culture. In order for these rules to have any meaning and authority at all for its citizens, they must be attached to a set of consequences.

CONSEQUENCES are (without judgment,) merely, THE NEXT SET OF CIRCUMSTANCES the individual finds themselves facing because of their decision to step beyond the boundaries and guidelines and break one of the established rules.

Consequences are intended to DETER the individual from making a choice to break the rule. BUT if the rule is broken, the consequence is intended to get a person to THINK TWICE about ever doing it again.

Parents rely heavily today on the use of consequences in their Family Culture to help their children make "better choices." They use consequences in an attempt to PREVENT children from doing something "wrong" or behaving "badly."

But if they do behave "badly," it is used to PUNISH them for making that "poor choice."

Consequences, implemented with judgment, will alter the feelings away from the child's experience of the actual consequence and refocus the feelings directly on the judgment itself by the parent and the reactive delivery of that judgment.

Since the Dr. Spock era until now, it seems that all of the parenting models have focused on "consequences to one's behavior." Natural or contrived consequences or positive and negative reward systems are used to establish a mechanism for children to "learn from their own mistakes, their own poor choices and their own failures."

Remember again, society has morphed into a SUCCESS AT ALL COST attitude that has been the standard for a long time. "Success at all cost" for our Family Culture, changes the experience of a consequence from the "next set of circumstances" we must face to "punishment" for the FAILURE that we let define us.

So, "punishment" MOTIVATES us toward success? NO, IT JUST DOESN'T WORK THAT WAY! Consequences are not designed to regulate us or motivate us. Consequences are designed only to HIGHLIGHT for us that the decision we made was NOT within the rules of the culture we are living in . . . Period!

Consequences become the next set of circumstances we face by the decision we made. If we make a decision that fits inside the set of rules, we have a certain reality we are facing. If we make a decision that we know does NOT fit inside the set of rules, we have a "consequential set of circumstances" to face.

So, the difficulty, then with the "rules and consequence model" we have been using thus far, is that if consequences are founded in judgment, they become punishment!

As long as parents "react in judgment" with "consequences," there will continue to be lack of character development in children today. Fear and avoidance of "punishment" forces children into "going underground."

As a part of a process of setting standards, expectations and rules, parents MUST leave space and room in the dynamic of the Family Culture for the "intention of the feelings" of the experience of the child.

FEELING. THOUGHT. DECISION. ACTION.

Parent your children to the "intention of their feelings" that lead them to their thoughts and their decisions to take action. Children, as we all do, have the ability to take into account the consequences that their actions may cause BEFORE they decide to act. They must know up front what the rules and consequences are, understand them, and then they are free to make their own decision.

The model of "consequences as punishment" we are using today, may be effective on some level to achieve "compliance" in our children. BUT punishment breeds fear and cannot address the goal of developing "self-regulation" in our children.

Remember, if nothing else, we as parents have the responsibility for parenting "self-regulation" so that we can have children grow up to be self-sufficient adults with a fully developed conscience. DELIVERY IS EVERYTHING!

Parents must deliver the expectations, guidelines, boundaries, rules and consequences with their children without "judgment." Parents must RESPOND, NOT REACT.

Parents must raise their children in a family culture that allows consequence to behavior to be truly only the "next set of circumstances" they face by their own actions and NOT a condemnation based on the emotional reaction from the parent.

There cannot be yelling; no creating consequences out of emotion, no judging children for their decision to step beyond the boundary. Just let the next set of circumstances unfold and trust the intention to feel the experience of the consequence the child will have.

The parenting moment here is to coach, educate and guide them through the experience by pursuing the child's voice to their experience and partnering around alternatives and solutions to the decisions that have been made by the child.

Think about it . . . Imagine speeding along the highway going 85 mph, in a 65 mph zone and getting stopped by the highway patrol? Imagine the officer walking up to your car and YELLING at you, reprimanding you for speeding? It just doesn't happen that way, does it?

The officer comes up to your vehicle, and asks you to step out of your car; Asks you if you knew how fast you were going; Asks you if you knew what the speed limit was, and then hands you your ticket (consequence) and tells you to drive more safely; (Coaches, educates and guides you through it.)

The patrol officer doesn't yell at you, doesn't lecture you, and doesn't emote at all. They assume the laws that govern us and the consequences to the laws broken are enough to create a "next set of circumstances" you may want to avoid.

It is then up to you, the individual, to decide whether to break the rules again, (speed in your car) and face the potential of another consequence.

I cannot tell you how many times I have posed the question to the kids who come to see me in my office, "What did you learn from your (speeding/ticket) experience?" And they have looked me straight me straight in the eyes and replied, "I should have done a better job not getting caught." . . . Scary!

The question becomes for each individual whether the consequence is something they wish to experience or do they relish in the freedom and ease to their life, living within the cultural rules.

CONSEQUENCES ALONE DO NOT STOP PEOPLE FROM MAKING DECISIONS THEY WANT TO MAKE!

Self-regulation requires a fully developed conscience and the freedom to experience whatever circumstance occurs from one's own voice, without the judgment of others.

So, let's set up a model of rules and consequences that promotes children making decisions without the fear of failure or condemnation if they make a mistake. We, as parents, can guide them to feel their experience and trust our children to learn from it. This requires a cultural structure with a set of rules, and consequences and a communication process without reaction. This allows for each individual to establish their own experience and their own intention to feel the moment of their experience, regardless of outcome.

FAMILY CONSTITUTION.

As we live in a society that requires both a federal and a state constitution to keep order and let each citizen live within their interpretation of the laws; family cultures, too, require a set of rules for the same purpose.

The FAMILY CONSTITUTION is an effective tool that parents can utilize to assist in maintaining order and holding to the standards of the culture they have developed. It allows parents to create the boundaries, the expectations and the set of rules they want their family to live by. It also allows the children to understand and identify with their parents' expectations while still having the ability to manage their own identity based on the rules established.

The parents become the "patrol officer" and the rules of the constitution become the guideline for "how fast we can drive on the highway."

It would be refreshing to approach our family culture with a structured set of rules and then let each member decide how they wish to make decisions accordingly. This removes the "reaction" and "judgment" and the parents' emotions associated with fear of the outcome of our children's choices.

Remember, the parents fear doesn't necessarily fully subside. But without judgment or reaction, and with a structured set of rules and consequences firmly in place in the culture, the parents' fear isn't interfering with child's process of learning and experiencing from life's decision making process.

When a child breaks a rule, they face the assigned or natural consequence. It becomes the child's choice to make. There is no yelling, no pleading, and no judgment.

Why? Because in order to learn to self-regulate with a conscience, a child needs to feel safe to try from their own interpretation of their feelings and experience of the moment.

Our children will decide if they speed in their car. They will decide if they steal from a store. They will decide if they get up and go to work. They will decide how they operate in their daily life because it is their moment to experience. It is the child's experience, voice, and identity. And, it will be the set of rules of the culture they live in; their "constitution" that will guide their decisions about their experience.

The rules, and more specifically their consequences, CAN only guide them as parents can only guide them. It will be their intentions of the feelings of their moment that will ultimately determine our children's choices.

Remember our example from early on in the book about the Rutgers University students who played a practical joke on their fellow student?

A couple of students decided to place a secret video they filmed of their friend kissing another young man in the privacy of his dorm room onto *You-Tube*™.

When the friend found out, he was so mortified and embarrassed, he committed suicide. Did these friends know "right from wrong?" Of course they did.

Did the students make choices based on the set of rules they are governed by?

No, they did not.

Did the consequences make a difference to their choices? No, they did not.

They made their choices from their internal voice and the intentions of their feelings. Their internal voice was not well enough developed to feel the moment of the true consequence of imposing into someone else's experience.

The Rutgers University students didn't think through the consequences of their actions, but, maybe more importantly, didn't "feel through" the consequences of their intentions.

Family constitutions establish a structure of boundaries and guidelines that will allow the child to experience their own moment within their family culture. Parents have an opportunity within the dynamics of this structure to guide, educate, coach and love their child while their child is experiencing their decisions (whatever they may be) unobstructed by reaction and judgment of others.

FAMILY CONSTITUTIONS
MUST BE FOUNDED IN RESPECT.

RESPECT is the attitude and process of HONORING someone or something through the intention to be KIND and MINDFUL of the other. Parents have the ominous task of creating an environment that promotes respect.

The Family Constitution can assist parents in accomplishing this task while also establishing an environment that will promote "self-regulation" by their children.

(Please remember what we talked about earlier in this book . . . Success and failure are equal and not to be judged as anything more than the "next set of circumstances" a child has to face, learn from and make their next decision from. No outcome can be too large or too small. They are just the punctuation of an experience and the beginning of the next. Children, like all of us will have many successes and failures throughout their lifetime. Teach them to experience them all without the fear of judgment.)

Once a Family Constitution is in place in the Family Culture, it becomes a living, working document that is open to revision and amendments as necessary for the development of the identity of the individual and the family as a whole.

THERE ARE THREE MAJOR SECTIONS TO A FAMILY CONSTITUTION

1. Respect of self
2. Respect of property
3. Respect of others

RESPECT OF SELF focuses on the rules, guidelines and boundaries that support the intention to "honor" mindfully and with kindness, one's "self," based on the expectations and standards in the family culture established by the parents.

Children are guided to "represent themselves" by their work ethic, manners, hygiene, delivery and choices, given the rules set forth in their constitution and the culture set forth by their parents.

RESPECT OF PROPERTY focuses on the rules, guidelines, and boundaries that support the intention to "honor" mindfully and with kindness the property or "things" in and around the environment, regardless of ownership.

Children are guided to taking "mindful care" and maintenance of their own things and honoring the boundaries around using things that belong to other people. They are also guided by the rules of where things reside and replacing these items once they are finished using them.

RESPECT OF OTHERS focuses on the rules, guidelines, and boundaries that support the intention to "honor" mindfully and with kindness, the feelings, thoughts and needs of the others in the environment.

Children are guided to "incorporate" the feelings, thoughts, and needs of other people into their own decision making process so that their choices do not affect adversely the other people around them. Let me show you how this works . . .

George and Sheila Dietrich have four children. Rory, the oldest, is 12-years-old and in 6th grade. Rory is a very good student and well liked by all his teachers in his middle school. He is, however, in a perpetual "power struggle" with his parents at home. Rory resents being the oldest and feels like he is constantly "victimized" by everyone in the family.

Mikey, the second oldest, is 8-years-old and in 3rd grade. Mikey struggles in school with academics but is well liked by both teachers and classmates. He is a very good athlete and plays sports year round.

Mikey is very charming and uses his charm with all the adults in his life. Mikey desperately wants to be close with his older brother, Rory, but Rory seems to despise everything about his brother Mike.

Sandy, is 6-years-old and in 1st grade. Sandy is a real "easy going kid" for her parents. She gets along with everyone in the family and is a "mother's little helper" with her younger sister, Millie. Sandy has many friends from all her extracurricular activities and has a very busy social calendar.

Millie is 2-years-old and will begin preschool in the fall. She is absolutely adorable, and is loved dearly and attended to by everyone in the family. She spends most of her time following her mother around during the day until Rory gets home from school. She then follows him around the rest of the day. Rory loves Millie but loves complaining more about her adoration of him.

The Dietrich Family has a very busy schedule with these four children, a large extended family and a very large group of friends. George Dietrich is a Certified Public Accountant who runs his own firm with fifty employees. George feels overwhelmed most of the time, with the stresses of running a business and being a father.

Sheila Dietrich is a stay at home mom and spends her time making sure that her family gets through the day. Sheila feels overwhelmed most of the time, with stresses of running a household and being a mother. George and Sheila Dietrich lived to get through the day focused on making it to the weekends, so that they can take a breath before doing it all over again. There is very little time for George and Sheila to be a couple. They both express feeling the loss of each other. They were once very good friends and a very romantic couple. But now they are proud parents of four children ranging in age from two to 12-years-old.

The Dietrichs have developed a family culture where the structure of the family dynamics is all held together by their attempts at "voice control." The rules and boundaries are set up as they go along and as the moment warrants. The consequences are created and decided upon as they go along.

There is no real consistency and structure the kids can count on and self-regulation is non-existent. Every dynamic in the family is reliant on judgment and reaction. Every family decision is made from a picture of what "everyone else" is doing.

(I must give the Dietrichs a break here, as most of the families I work with in my practice are exactly like this family.)

You can only imagine the noise, and tumult that goes on in a family where "order" is managed by the reaction and judgment. Chaos becomes the only order a family like the Dietrichs' can rely on. Weekends becomes the finish line of five long, hard days of "getting through," and the "intention to feel" one's moment is replaced with "defending one's position" and survival.

George Dietrich has a very stressful job. When he arrives home at night, he wants calm and order and never seems to experience it. He dreads coming home and what kind of explosion he may encounter. So, he spends his day "putting out fires" and he spends his evenings doing the same thing.

During the day, with his employees and clients, he "responds;" at night with his family, he "reacts."

Sheila is a very "hands on" mother and is in constant motion with her children.

She is so "hands on" that making up the rules and the consequences as she moves along through the day, feels necessary and important to her identity as a mother.

She believes when you have four young children at these ages, this is just how it is and when they all grow up a little, things will improve.

Sheila tries very hard to provide George with the experience he is looking for when he walks in from work, but doesn't believe it's possible or realistic to achieve.

"With four children, I don't know what he expects?" She has been known to say.

(Parenting "on the run", with no structured set of rules and consequences, makes it impossible to provide children with a safe place to have their voice and experience; their moment WITHOUT being in reaction to their parents.)

George and Sheila Dietrich are a loving, committed couple and will survive this period in their life. However, the goal of having children and the parenting experience, is not merely just to survive.

The goal of being a parent is to experience the joy of your relationship with your children; while coaching, guiding and loving them from the sidelines of their own experience and still enjoying your own moment.

The Dietrichs were not enjoying much anymore. George and Sheila Dietrich bickered in my office about the same argument they have at home every night. George believes if Sheila would get better control of the kids, and was more organized at in the house, he would come home to a calmer environment. Sheila believes that there is nothing she can do differently and that George has to accept the family situation they are living in.

I nudged my way into the bickering and asked . . . "I wonder how the kids would feel if you guys stopped yelling at them?"

"If we stop yelling at them all chaos would let loose!" George reacted instantly.

Everyone stopped, realized what George had just said and burst out into laughter.

(I love the Dietrichs. They have a great sense of humor and are willing to laugh at themselves. It sure makes it easier to help people make changes when they are willing to lighten things up.)

"How could there be any more chaos than there already is?" he quickly followed up.

"Exactly. You see, you are in a constant power struggle with one another, with the kids and with the circumstance, itself. You are reacting emotionally to everything around you." I tried to suggest gently.

"What else can we do? We have four children." Sheila said defensively.

"First of all, you guys are awesome parents. You are here and you are willing to make things healthier. That's half the battle. Also, you are best friends and it's clear that you love one another very much. HOWEVER, you have a family culture that has all the expectations and standards in place but no structure to allow the kids to maneuver around in their own life . . . which means there is no room for each of you to maneuver around in your own life." I explained.

"What do you suggest?" George asked as Sheila took a deep breathe and sighed.

"Let's start with creating a Family Constitution. A Family Constitution is a set of rules and consequences that all the members of your family live by . . . just like we all live by a set of laws that govern each of us. Then we will teach the kids what the rules and their consequences are and let them try and follow the set of rules without you managing their every move. At that point we will declare to every one of your kids, that you guys will stop yelling, lecturing or judging them. You two won't care if they follow the rules or not. You are just going to coach them, teach them, guide them, and love them. If they choose to break the rules, you will enforce the consequence and move along." I boldly said.

It was silent for at least three or four minutes, which felt like forever.

"Really?" George said. "No way," Sheila added

"Really . . . yes way!" I said, then adding . . . "You guys need to put order and calm into you life experience. You AND your children need this. Every culture of people must live feeling safe, feeling heard, and feeling valued. Otherwise, people feel the need to fight back or get out somehow. We don't want anyone getting out and you are already fighting back." I concluded.

"Let's try it. What do you have to lose?" I asked.

"Okay, let's try it! What do you think, Sheila?" George asked with enthusiasm.

"Why not . . . it's not working this way!" Sheila responded.

So, after more direction and explanation, the Dietrichs left with their homework assignment. They were going out on a date alone with each other, and their laptop. They were going to draft The Dietrich Family Constitution based on Respect of Self, Property, and Others.

The trick for them was to draft something that not only spoke to the set of rules and consequences, but also took into account the different developmental ages of their children. The following is what they finally settled upon to begin their new structure . . . .

(Remember, the Family Constitution is a living, working document, intended to be modified as necessary as the family grows and changes.)

THE DIETRICH FAMILY CONSTITUTION:

• RESPECT OF SELF

1. Hygiene . . . Shower or bathe everyday without argument; brush teeth each morning and before bed.
2. Chores . . . Take charge of your assigned chore and complete it each day with one reminder by a parent. (Millie will be assisted with her chore by a parent and must do it when told.)
3. Language . . . No cursing or name calling.
4. Homework . . . If you have homework, do it right when you get home without being told by a parent.

• CONSEQUENCE

Loss of all electronics (including television, computer, iPod, telephone, etc.) for the rest of day. If rule continues to be broken, loss will continue for the next day, and so on. If verbally defiant when getting the consequence . . . Lose participation in the next extra curricular activity. Continued defiance will result in loss of freedom to play with friends . . . duration determined by parents.

• RESPECT OF PROPERTY

1. Your own things . . . Clean up after yourself, replace what you take out, where it belongs, clean up your room each evening before bedtime, have a home for all personal items and keep the item there when not using it.
2. Someone else's things . . . Do not take something that does not belong to you without permission. When borrowing something, handle it with care and get it back to the person you borrowed it from.
3. Family property . . . Handle with care all the items that the family uses together, such as furniture, kitchen items, electronics.

• CONSEQUENCES

Loss of all electronics (including television, computer, iPod, telephone, etc.) for the rest of the day. If rule continues to be broken, loss will continue for the next day and so on. If verbally defiant when getting the consequence . . . Lose participation in the next extracurricular activity. Continued defiance will result in loss of freedom to play with friends . . . duration determined by parents.

• RESPECT OF OTHERS

1. No violence . . . no hitting, pinching, pushing, or touching someone else without their permission.
2. No verbal disrespect . . . no teasing, no name calling and no annoying

noises directed toward someone else.

3. Manners . . . say "please and thank you," help when requested, stay out of each other's business unless asked.

• CONSEQUENCES . . . Loss of all electronics (including television, computer, iPod, telephone, etc.) for the rest of the day. If rule continues to be broken, loss will continue for the next day and so on. If verbally defiant when getting the consequence . . . Lose participation in the next extra curricular activity. Continued defiance will result in loss of freedom to play with friends . . . duration determined by parents.

As you can see, The Dietrich Family Constitution is not a perfect document that includes every possible behavior and consequence experienced by all of their four children. This is not "rocket science" and the Family Constitution does not have to be complicated. It does, however, have to be consistently followed and upheld.

The true difficulty parents have with the Family Constitution is believing in the PROCESS and remaining CONSISTENT! Parents MUST follow through with governing the structure and letting their child self-regulate within the process.

Often times, parents start these tools with great promise and then, over time, old patterns of reaction come into play and the Family Constitution becomes history.

The Dietrichs started out slowly with a few general, yet important rules in each category of RESPECT.

George and Sheila wanted to be mindful of their children not feeling overwhelmed by too many details. They also wanted to set up a structure of rules that were adaptable to each age group of their four children. And they, themselves, wanted to be ready, to "respond" and stop "reacting" to the actions of their kids.

The Dietrich Family needed to be ready to let the structure govern the culture and let their children navigate their identity within the family culture.

The Dietrich Family Constitution had been established by George and Sheila, out of a desperate need for order, relief, and the truly desperate need to find a sense of peace and joy in the family experience. The set of rules and consequences they created were general enough for all their children and yet specific to what they held important, RESPECT, and what the kids hold important, FREEDOM, as represented by such preferences as their electronics, activities and friends.

George and Sheila Dietrich called a family meeting to discuss with the kids the new approach to the Family Culture.

Every member sat around the kitchen table with great interest. They unveiled the Family Constitution with its rules and consequences. They enlisted Sandy and Millie the day before to create a bright and beautiful Family Constitution on a large piece of construction paper. It was very creative with pictures of every member of the family drawn on the document. Even their dog, Oreo, had a place for her picture.

Rory sat next to his brother and seemed angry at the need for the meeting. He and his brother behaved as they always do, poking, pinching and prodding each other, without a whole lot of attention to what was being said.

Sandy and Millie were both so proud of their artistic efforts and were attentively engaged in every word George said to explain the new process.

For George, the tension kept building and the Family Meeting was beginning to feel like every other experience around the kitchen table. He was getting so frustrated and angry that the very meeting that was going to change the culture was exactly like the culture.

You see, it takes a long time to change culture and you cannot expect children to just change because you say "change."

George took a deep breathe, looked over to Sheila with a sad expression on his face, but continued on and finished his little speech.

George took the first step towards change . . . he did NOT react! Family

Constitutions don't have to be serious pieces of legislature. It is a family tool used for and by everyone to understand what the guidelines are in the Family Culture and what will happen if they don't follow the rules.

The PROCESS of implementing and following the Family Constitution will prove to be much more important than the content or display of the document. Every child is asked to embrace and "own" the rules and learn to regulate themselves without the need for parental reaction. The parents are asked to STOP reacting and ONLY respond with guidance, coaching and love. The Family Constitution becomes the boundaries around the "practice field" of the family life and the parents are asked to have the courage to get off the field and now "coach" from the sidelines.

I met with George and Sheila Dietrich after a few weeks of the family adjusting to the new approach and the Family Constitution. Here is what they reported . . .

"It's not working." George said defiantly.

"What do you mean by 'not working'?" I asked.

"Rory has gotten worse than ever and I can't stop fighting with him. He hit me the other night!" He explained.

"Do you believe in this new process? Do you believe in the approach of teaching your children to self-regulate?" I asked.

"I guess so, but you said this would create order and it seems that we have more chaos." He said settling down.

"Sheila, tell me about the other kids?" I asked trying to get a more complete picture.

"Well, let me see . . . Millie loves the Family Constitution and asks me everyday whether she is doing a good job, but she's two. Sandy is always my little 'mom' and tries real hard to remind everyone else what the rules are. I am working with her to focus on her, only. But she loves the idea of having less yelling in the family. Mikey tries real hard to follow the rules and has had a few consequences each week, but he, too, is trying. Actually, everyone is trying except Rory and . . . frankly, George.

"It is much better around the house up until dinner time, then it's like it used to be. I really try not to react, and just give out the consequence, but it's so hard," she explained calmly.

"So let's talk about Rory, for a moment. You see, changing culture is really scary.

"It threatens the identity and roles people are used to playing in their family culture. In fact, there is always a kid who will 'ratchet' up the stakes to force their parent back into their old role of a 'reactor.'

"Rory is trying with all his might to keep you guys yelling and reacting. It's what he's used to," I explained.

"So, what do you want us to do?" George re-engaged.

"You have to believe in the process, have a huge amount of patience and commit that no matter how high Rory ratchets up the stakes, you will remain NEUTRAL and NOT REACT. You will RESPOND by giving him the next circumstance his behavior puts in front of him . . . keep giving him the consequences and don't get emotionally involved. Stop being so 'mad' at him for what he is choosing to do." I answered.

"How long will it take for Rory to 'get it'?" George asked.

"As long as it takes . . . believe in him . . . and believe in the process and the structure.

The real question you need to be asking is . . . 'How long will it take for YOU to get it?' He won't get it until you do," I concluded.

Sheila and George looked at one another and Sheila reached out to hold George's hand. He initially hesitated and then reached out for her as well.

We scheduled a follow-up meeting to this conversation for a month later. The Dietrichs went home fully committed to the plan . . . no more reaction, trust the structure and the process and most importantly, TRUST THEIR CHILDREN to eventually "get it." The month flew by for all of us. The Dietrichs visually looked like an entirely different couple as they took their seats on the sofa in my inner office. (It's such an interesting thing about human beings that they operate in such ritualistic ways. George and Sheila, like every other person who comes to my office sits it the same place every time they are here! I have always found that to be an interesting observation of people. Sorry, just a random thought!)

"Well, what's new guys?" I asked. (For those of you who are reading this and have had the experience to sit on my sofa, I know you are smiling right now. You see, I am known for opening my meetings with "What's new?" It's just one of those things.)

"We want to report that everything is new. Things feel so much better. I'm not saying that we are perfect at this, but the kids are following the rules mostly and when they don't, we just give them another consequence. I think Mikey is in the lead!" Sheila began.

"What do you mean in the lead?" I asked curiously.

"The kids asked if we could modify our Family Constitution process a little and keep track each week as to who has the most and least amount of consequences. Kind of a competition," George joined in.

"Sounds awesome. Great idea. When you have kids this age, there is often a natural competition and you are using it positively. What about Rory?" I responded.

"Rory and I had a long talk and we agreed to help each other follow the rules and stop fighting with each other. I made a commitment to him that I will not react. He actually thought I hated him!" George said in tears.

"Sounds like you are well on your way to changing the culture and having order in your family. I'm so proud of all of you! It takes courage to make these changes. Good for you!" I said, feeling genuinely excited for them.

"We would like to focus on our relationship with you, now that we are following the new structure as a family. I am so proud of George for how hard he is trying and actually proud of me too for what we are accomplishing." Sheila put out there.

"Just remember, the real challenge now with the new Family Culture and the Family Constitution is being consistent and making it to the 'new normal.' It is easy to go back to what you were doing before if you are not conscious and resolved to make this the new family dynamic. Let's schedule a time to talk about the two of you." I concluded with a great sense of pride.

Changing the Family Culture and its dynamics takes great resolve and a constant attention to the new standard of the new "normal."

Parents cannot give up on the process, the structure or believing in their children.

Parents build their structure, change their reactions to responses and step aside to coach, guide and love them through their experience.

Rituals, such as the Family Meeting discussed in the Dietrich family story, will assist parents and children in embracing the new dynamics and culture as their new identity. More about RITUALS in the next chapter.

Until then . . .

CHAPTER EIGHT

Rituals, Rituals, Rituals

Rituals help create identity. Think about it . . . If you put down your book, walk outside and take a random polling of 20 people walking by, (assuming you have 20 people walking by,) and ask the following questions . . .

"What day do Christians typically go to church each week?" 20 out of the 20 will answer . . . "Sunday," . . . of course!

OR . . . "What food is typically eaten on Thanksgiving Day each year?" 20 out of 20 will answer . . . "Turkey!" Again, of course.

Why? Because these rituals have been around consistently for so long that you don't even have to participate in these special days yourself to know their identity.

Because RITUALS DO HELP CREATE IDENTITY!

People seem to thrive in the rituals of our lives. The rituals add meaning to the experience we have as something valuable enough to make us want to do it consistently, again and again.

When we designate a specific time and space to honor the worth of our experience, it then becomes something that defines our experience. We identify with our preference and we prioritize our experience.

We feel a level of safety when we know what and when things are supposed to happen and where things are supposed to be. And as I have written numerous times before in this book . . . a parent's role is to create a safe place for their child to experience the intention of their feelings. Rituals provide such a safe place in the Family Culture.

I remember telling a story on my radio show, *The Parent Coach*, (Catchy title don't you think?) about a woman who wrote an article on ritual and identity. The story goes like this . . .

When she was a little girl in the 1970's, Jane was invited to a birthday party at a classmate's house. Her little friend, Karen had a big fancy party in her backyard and when it was time for cake, her mother brought out this new fangled looking dessert . . . an ice cream cake.

All the little girls were "wowed" by the beauty and tastes of this brand new type of birthday cake. You see, they had never seen nor tasted a Dairy Queen ice cream cake before! It was brand new!

When Jane went home after Karen's birthday party, she went on and on to her mother about the wonders of the ice cream cake. She pleaded with her mother to get her an ice cream cake for her birthday which was coming up later that month.

After much pleading, Jane's mother promised to have an ice cream cake at her next birthday party. And so she did.

The party was in full bloom in Jane's backyard and it was finally time for the birthday cake; the birthday "ice cream" cake.

Family and friends gathered around Jane, waiting for her mother to walk outside with the prettiest birthday cake from Dairy Queen that you could possibly wish for.

Jane's mother walked outside with the cake, with candles lit and ready to be blown out (first making a wish, of course.)

Jane took one look at her cake, let out a cry and ran to her room in tears for the rest of the day, never to return to her own birthday party. What happened?

Jane's mother walked outside carrying a one gallon square brick of Neapolitan ice cream that had been removed from its container, placed on a platter with blazing candles inserted on top.

This experience became the inside joke of the family and thus the new birthday ritual for everyone in Jane's family. (This family had a great sense of humor and saw the value in identifying with this very funny experience.)

From that day on, if it was your birthday, you were going to get a one pound brick of Neapolitan ice cream, on a platter with candles on top.

Today, the little girl is a grown woman with children of her own, and the tradition continues.

As parents develop their family culture, it is the experience that they value that creates the rituals, and it's the rituals in their life that "identifies" their experience.

Nobody in this little girl's family "scripted" out the experience that happened one summer afternoon at her birthday party. Yet that experience became such an important moment for this family that they made it a priority to replicate.

The family "ritualized" the experience as a way to put special meaning to the specific identity of family birthday celebrations.

Do you remember in the chapter on Family Culture, I mentioned my mother, Goldie's famous sweet and sour meatballs that she made every year at the Jewish New Year? Now THAT was a ritual that identified the holiday for me!

Not only do I remember it happening every year, I can still feel the importance of the "meatball" experience because my parents made it a priority to have them as part of the holiday menu every year.

As a little boy and a young adult, I looked forward to the smell and tastes of sweet and sour meatballs at the "High Holidays." Even today, I remember so vividly those holidays and the experience of anticipating Goldie's meatballs. It was a ritual that defined our family during that time. Goldie's sweet and sour meatballs, every year at the Jewish New Year became a ritual that helped create our family identity.

One night, Linda and I went to our friend Michael's house to pay our respects for the death of his mother. All of our friends were there doing the same thing, and as usual with this group, there was plenty of food out for everyone to enjoy (ritual).

Displayed along with all the chicken, brisket, potatoes and vegetables, there was a noodle salad that nobody present had ever recognized as a typical addition to the table's offerings. I overheard our friend describe the noodle salad with such pride and tears in his eyes, "That was the noodle salad recipe my mother used to make for parties. I love that salad! It makes me think of her," Michael said with the complex mixture of joy and sadness one has during moments like that.

I caught a glimpse of the Family Culture that Michael's family experienced with one taste of a noodle salad, and the reminiscing it brought to Michael's memory. This was one of *his* rituals that helped create his family identity.

Parents today find it difficult to maintain the same consistency in their Family Culture that our parents were able to create. With the pressure to be active and involved like "everyone else," the ability to maintain consistency in the Family Culture is almost impossible.

The danger here is that if parents don't develop the priority and consistency to create the rituals they wish to identify themselves with, the chaos and tumult of the day and week will become the ritual experience that define the family and its members. This was the case with the Dietrichs from the previous chapter when I first met them.

The process of developing their Family Constitution was so important not only to put order in their home, but to prioritize to their children the standard of behavior that defines them as a family and as individuals.

But it is the RITUALIZING of the family experience that transitions the Family Constitution from a new "exercise" into a consistent priority of the Family Cultural experience.

Parents, like the Dietrichs' are very capable of understanding and implementing something new into their Family Culture, but finding the rituals necessary to maintain the new approach and make something "new" into the "norm" is another story.

I cannot tell you how many families start out trying something new to improve their family experience, only to fall back into the same old patterns they are attempting to replace. This speaks to the power of rituals, doesn't it?

Healthy or not, rituals form patterns in a culture that people come to expect, anticipate and hold onto tightly as it becomes a part of who they are and how they operate.

This speaks to the RESOLVE necessary to change the patterns and rituals that are in place with something new and maintain the consistency, and repetition required to make it the new ritual that the family identifies with.

A strong commitment is necessary to make something new a strong enough priority to the Family Culture to become a RITUAL. (There have been many Family Constitutions thrown into the waste basket because the resolve just wasn't there to consistently make the new experience the ritualized experience.)

Let me share with you some personal examples of rituals that created identity for my family . . .

Linda and I found each other later in life. (Although, it truly feels as if nothing ever happened before I met her. That's just the kind of love we share!)

Quick side note . . . We both wish that we would have found one another when we were much younger, but we recognize that each of us had to go through what life experiences we went through in order to have found one another at all. I am the luckiest man alive!

Hard as it is for me to fathom, there were indeed life moments before I met Linda . . .

Lizzy, Justin and I have had many rituals that defined us as they were growing up. As an example, I would create Friday "date night," once or twice per month, or more, and take each of them to a movie and dinner, to spend special one on one time.

I worked crazy hours in my practice back then, so this gave us special time together that would help define our relationship. We started this ritual when they were young, and it continued on until they reached the middle school years.

I knew I had a limited time frame with them for this ritual, because once a kid hits middle school, they would rather be with their friends at the movie, rather than their father.

Although, you may be able to squeeze out a dozen more "dates" or so if you are willing to include their friends in on an activity as well. In fact, you begin the transition from being their "date," to being their "chauffeur" pretty quickly, which is a healthy twist and was just fine with me. (Remember, it's their growing up experience, not mine. I had my meatballs!)

Lizzy was a USS swimmer from age 8 to age 12, and practiced four or five days a week. Unfortunately she had to retire from the sport at age 12. We were driving home from a swim practice when we were hit from behind by a drunk driver. We were lucky to be alive, but the injury to her back wouldn't enable her to continue swimming at such a high level of performance. Four to five days of practice, swim meets every weekend, and then it all stopped at the ripe old age of 12! Talk about ritual creating identity! What happens to the identity when the ritual stops? (It was a tough time, to say the least.)

We carpooled with the girls from her swim team to all of the practices so that each family could maintain some balance at home while the girls pursued their passion. They worked so hard, juggling school work, their swimming and all of life's other expectations they had to fulfill.

I wanted them to celebrate their sacrifice and hard work, so when it was my day each week to drive carpool, we, of course developed our own ritual that defined *our* carpool identity.

Lizzy and I would pick up three other girls from around our neighborhood and head to the swimming pool at the local high school. I would sit and wait, (as many parents would do,) bringing paperwork or reading with me to pass the time. (Have you ever sat in a hot, muggy natatorium watching swimmers do laps for two hours? Oh my goodness, there were times I would beg for someone to just shoot me and put me out of my misery!)

All the girls rushed to get ready with anticipation, because they knew what to expect . . . they knew the Dembo carpool ritual.

Once the girls were in the car and clicked their seatbelts, they turned the music up as loud as we could get away with in traffic, and then, of course the singing began. The trip through the Dairy Queen drive thru was sure to follow.

. . . Everybody knew what to expect. They knew what music they wanted to hear. They all sat in their place in the car. And they all ordered the same thing at the DQ.

I am sure today, if you asked any one of these girls, who are all young women now, they would tell you the stories of the "Dembo carpool ritual."

Rituals help create identity. They bring meaning, priority and purpose to an experience.

There was a time in my life when I was living alone with Justin in a small house on Sun Flower Court. (Two males living together on a street named Sun Flower Court; I took a little razzing for that, but luckily I was pretty comfortable with my identity.)

Lizzy was away finishing college at Truman State University but would come home to us frequently on weekends. I am happy to say that my children and I have always had a very close relationship.

As with most families of divorce, we struggled a bit through the changes in the family identity after their mother and I divorced. When family identity changes, the children can often feel adrift and not have anything to assign their identity to anymore.

It's like opening a wound without any type of bandage or stitches to close it back up to heal. The family as they once knew it had changed, and now there were two family cultures to build while healing the wounds from the loss of the original Family Culture itself. I could sense how lost we all felt.

Even though we were constantly processing their thoughts and feelings, my kids didn't feel that safety net anymore of what to expect in their Family

Culture. There were no longer Family Culture rituals that identified them. They were replaced with a schedule of visitation, especially Justin who still lived at home. This was a sad time in our lives.

It's emotionally dangerous for children to have the rituals that have defined them replaced with the ritual of "visitation," without new Family Cultural rituals that allow for a new identity for their Family. (This is unfortunately a very common dynamic for children of divorce, and the sooner parents create new rituals their children can hold onto, the better.)

Justin moved in with me full time fairly quickly, as his mother went away to school in Florida. Right away, I declared a non-negotiable ritual . . . Sunday night family dinner at 6:15 p.m. Whoever was in town, family dinner was served at 6:15 p.m. and the location was to be determined from week to week. (After all, I could only barbecue so often!)

The weeks were busy for all of us, but come Sunday evening, we were together no matter what, enjoying the moment of our experience.

Why 6:15 p.m. you may wonder? I wanted it to be an odd time to give it even more identifiable characteristics and something the kids would enjoy talking about. And they certainly did.

Both kids wrapped themselves immediately around this ritual and anticipated it each week with joy. Often times, I would hear from Lizzy that she would want to come into town and bring friends to our Sunday night family dinner. Justin would also invite his friends, or "girlfriend of the week" (middle school and high school . . . you know how it is).

But mostly, it was us . . . the family who attended. And this was the beginning of a new identity for our new Family Culture.

Why? Because it took the pain and chaos out of the family wound and replaced it with an intention to feel the moment of being a family.

As Linda came into our life, she joined in on Sunday Night Family Dinner as well. Linda, too, understood the need for ritual and its healing powers as it creates the safety of consistency and anticipation. She helped us enhance the rituals of our family identity.

From Sunday Night Family Dinner came "Taco Tuesdays." Linda makes a "mean" Mexican meal, featuring great tacos and enchiladas!

Linda, Justin, and I (with guest appearances by Linda's son, Jonathan) would have this amazing Mexican meal, and watch American Idol. (Linda made us watch it . . . really!)

Sunday Night Family Dinner remains an important ritual in our blended family today. Everyone in the family . . . Lizzy, Jeremy, Rachel, Justin, and Adam, Linda and I, along with regular guest appearances by Uncle Mike, (Linda's brother) all embrace the ritual. If you are in town, it is a given you are included at our Sunday Family Dinner.

Rituals help create identity.

If you go by the stories and examples given thus far in this chapter, you might conclude that the secret to a ritual is food. Not exactly. There are many effective and important rituals parents can consider for their Family Culture. Feeding your family just happens to be one ritual you can count on everyday of your life.

FAMILY MEALS.

The Family meal, historically, has been a time when families come together to eat, talk about the day, and plan for upcoming events. As the family dynamic has changed through the last 50 years, so has the occurrence of the Family Meal.

Today, in a culture that has "morphed" into a "success at all cost" world with the pressure of doing what "everyone else" is doing, the everyday family meal time has been replaced with fast food eaten out of a bag on the way to soccer practice. The Family Meal ritual has died an unfortunate death.

Well, it is time to bring the Family Meal time back to the Family Culture and prioritize the time to sit, nourish, and converse as a family.

I recognize that it may be difficult to bring the family to the table every night of the week as we may have done so 50 years ago. Parents need to decide how important the Family Meal is as a ritual in creating a safe space and time to experience the family identity.

Once the parent makes that a priority, they can schedule in these family meals, and reorganize the family culture around them. It's not going to be an easy task to implement something new into a ritualized environment that currently doesn't have it as a priority. Often, something has to be deleted in order to have something added, which will initially create resistance and emotion.

Parents must have the RESOLVE to make the change happen. They have to believe in the value of the Family Meal experience and have to be willing to say goodbye to whatever they are taking away, even if "everyone else" is doing it.

Parents must choose when and how often these meals will be honored. Although the importance of the family meal is not necessarily in the actual meal itself, it is in the modeling of the values the parents are trying to express . . . that taking time out, being together peacefully, each member having a role, each member having their own voice, and everyone experiencing the sense of being one family unit is a priority over all other activities.

The Family Meal experience can include ritualized roles for all members. The menu setting and grocery shopping, the setting the table and clean up, and of course, the food preparation are all valuable moments that can include each and every family member, regardless of age. These roles can be ritualized and become a part of the members' identity in the experience of the Family Meal.

Children are not guests to these events. They can be active participants, taking an active, prideful interest in the quality of the meal and the quality of the experience. The Family Meal is a perfect "safe place" for children to experience the intentions of their feelings, IF . . . the parents are responding and not reacting, and a set of rules are in place to expect each member to behave accordingly or experience the related consequence.

The Family Meal for the Dietrich family, if you remember from last chapter, was a painful breeding ground for the chaos and pain. It was a complete "reaction-fest" of emotions each member was stuck in as the ritual of their meal.

The father, George, dreaded coming home to his family at dinner time. Sheila Dietrich felt so discouraged because she worked so hard to create a nice family meal, only to watch the whole thing fall apart night after night. Their four children felt "comfortably uncomfortable" in the chaos, because chaos WAS the ritual of the meal that they had come to expect. It had become their identity.

With a set of rules and consequences in place, and with a dynamic of "response" rather than "reaction" from the Dietrichs', the Family Meal has gone from this "reaction-fest" it once was, to a safe place for each member to experience the intention of their feelings and express these feelings accordingly.

The Dietrichs will tell you today that the Family Meal is an important priority in their lives, and have a strong resolve to have these meals two or three times per week.

The Family Meal time is an important ritual for parents to consider making a priority. It can be a "natural time-out" in the week for family members to put aside their individual agenda, become a part of the family unit and experience the identity of the whole group.

Families who live with these rituals will give testimony to the importance these meals have for them not only as a family, but also for their individual identity.

Family Meals give the individual a place to take a pause, and share their view of the world and get feedback from the views of others who love them.

Without judgment and reaction, it's a safe place to be coached by committee, from the people who know you best.

FAMILY MEETINGS.

The Family Meeting is a time set aside each week for the whole family to sit down and review the upcoming schedule of activities and expectations, review the set of rules and consequences, (The Family Constitution) and allow each member to share thoughts, suggestions and concerns.

Think about a well run business or organization. Typically, every Monday morning, there is a staff meeting scheduled for the entire team to sit down and review the week's workload, goals and expectations. This provides order in the organization and a feeling of safety for each staff member to do their job with a sense of confidence and freedom because they know what is being expected.

The FAMILY MEETING is designed for the very same purpose. It gives the family a designated time each week to review the expectations, schedule and goals for the week. The Family Meeting, like the Family Meal, can be a safe place for each member to learn to express their voice and for the family to learn to operate as a unit.

Unlike the Family Meal, where it may be easier to prioritize because everyone needs to be fed, the Family Meeting takes great resolve by the parents to prioritize.

Parents must decide that they find value in having a meeting each week and making that experience a ritual irreplaceable by other events.

Many families find that they can tie the Family Meeting to the Family Meal. Often times the family meeting can follow the end of the meal.

Say hello to the Walsh family . . .

The Walsh Family lives in a small town about 60 minutes from St Louis, Missouri. They are a prominent family in this small town of 20,000 people. Steven and Rose own and operate the largest hardware store in town. They are leaders in their church and are members of the Board of one of the local banks. Steven and Rose Walsh have two sons; Steven Jr., 16-years-old and Carson, 10-years-old.

The Walsh boys are as prominent in their community as their parents. Steven Jr. is a very good athlete and a very good student. He is being recruited by major colleges to play baseball and plays for two select teams as well as his high school.

Did I mention that Steven Jr., (everyone calls him Stevey,) is quite handsome and very popular with the ladies?

Carson, Stevey's younger brother, is a brilliant student academically and a star on his soccer team. He sings in his church choir and plays the piano with great expertise. This is just one of those families that *seems* to have everything going for them.

Except for one thing . . . no one seems to get along and everyone fights disrespectfully with each other behind closed doors. The "picture" of this family is amazing. The "truth" of this family is painful.

Steven and Rose brought their children with them when they came to my office for their first visit. I usually request for the parents to come alone, but they ignored that request and brought the boys with them.

"We cannot have the disrespect from these two boys," said Steven.

"We don't know where we went wrong with them, but they seem to hate us," added Rose.

Both boys remained silent. (Not unusual under these circumstances. I'm not sure I would say anything either if I were them.)

"I'm not sure what you mean . . . They hate you?" I questioned.

"We have to tell them what they need to do all the time and instead of just doing it, they mouth back at us with hatred. It's unbelievable." Rose exclaimed.

"Do they finally do what you ask?" I inquired.

"Sometimes, but that's not the point." Steven said with frustration at my line of questioning.

"What's the point, then?" I asked with frustration at Steven's arrogance.

"The point is, they talk back to their parents and it's not permissible," he explained.

"Do you know why they are so mad at you?" I asked, thinking that was the next obvious question.

"No, that's why we came to you! I thought you had a good reputation. Are you sure you know what you are doing?" Steven yelled. (Ahhh, I just love my job, some days.)

"Mr. Walsh, if you talk to your boys the same way you are talking to me, I might talk back too." I replied calmly.

Stevey and Carson began to chuckle under their breath. "You boys think this is funny?" Rose began to attack.

I knew this family needed me to take control before it got way out of hand.

"I'm sorry Mr. Walsh. I know you feel desperate and worried about the boys. I promise that if you don't feel you are getting anywhere here with me, I will help you find someone you are more comfortable with. But follow me here for a minute," I interjected.

"Okay, but where are you going with this?" he asked.

"You have a beautiful family and you should be very proud of what you and Mrs. Walsh have accomplished. Did you know that the best indicator of how you are doing as a parent is how your children behave in another parent's home?" I added.

"Really? We hear all the time from other parents that both of our boys are wonderful with them," Rose said with relief.

"Then why do they behave this way at home?" Rose went on to ask.

I continued on. "Your family home is their "practice field" for what your boys do out there in the world. So you must be doing something right. The disrespect displayed by ALL of you is the issue, isn't it? So we have to figure out a way to attend to that issue."

I turned my attention to the boys. "Come on now, I need your help here. Will either of you help me figure out why there is so much disrespect going on?" I urged with great emphasis.

Both boys started talking at the same time and then Carson backed off and let his older brother explain.

"They bark orders at us all day long. They never stop and nothing is ever good enough. We follow the rules for the most part, but they just won't leave us alone," Stevey said with tears in his eyes.

"Are you guys willing to stop being so reactive and disrespectful?" I asked.

"I knew this would be about us," Stevey said.

"No, I think you are ALL being disrespectful. All of you. Your parents seem to micromanage two really good kids when they don't need to, which, by the way feels disrespectful to you both, as if you get no credit for being good kids. And you guys both react rudely, thinking that will get your point across. But it doesn't, does it? Nothing changes and each of you is unhappy," I explained cautiously as to make sure all family members were getting this point.

"So what's the solution? We are not going to lessen our standards. That's who we are," Rose inserted into the conversation.

"I think you need organization and ritual wrapped around your rules and expectations. Then, there will be no need for the disrespect," I answered.

"What?" asked Carson, finally getting into the action.

"Yeah . . . what?" Steven inquired.

I knew we were headed in the right direction because for the first time in the hour, a parent and a kid were on the same side of the question.

"Let's start with homework for all of you. (The boys groaned when they heard the word "homework," as every kid does.) Here is what I need from you guys. Stevey and Carson, I want you to take the rules your parents have for you and put them into a Family Constitution. Write the rules under these three categories, and then come up with what you think the consequences are if you break the rules."

1. Respect of Self
2. Respect of Property
3. Respect of Others

"Email me if you guys need help, but do not ask your parents."

"Mom and Dad, I want you to find a time each week to have a Family Meeting and come up with a weekly agenda. Steven, you have staff meetings at work don't you? These are just as important to your family as those are to your business. Keep it simple but make sure all the issues you badger the kids with are included in the agenda so you won't have to micromanage them during the rest of the week," I rattled off quickly as to not be interrupted.

"Okay, so a Family Constitution is the list of rules and consequences my parents have for us and you want them under those Respect categories, right?" asked Stevey.

"Right. My feeling is that if your parents knew that you had the list of rules and expectations, and they backed off and were not allowed to "badger you," they would see that you guys would manage yourself quite nicely," I said confidently.

"Oh my god, this is awesome! Yes, that's what we have been trying to tell them," Stevey yelled out as he got a high five from Carson.

"Yeah, but you don't have a right, no matter how much they harp on you, to treat them the way you have been treating them," I followed.

"And your parents need a time when they can meet with you about these issues and feel like their team, their family, are all "on the same page." That's the need for the Family Meeting. It is a time to be accountable, to follow your parents' agenda, and for each of you to speak kindly about the issues in the family that need attending to," I explained.

"This is brilliant. This is exactly what we do at work and it makes total sense to me," Steven said with a smile.

"Okay, you boys have to get started on this constitution," harped Rose.

"Rose, no! You are not allowed to do that anymore. You can bring it up at the next Family Meeting, which will be here in my office, in two weeks." I headed her off kindly at the pass.

Everyone giggled nervously at what Rose just did. It just became clear that making these changes were not as easy as it sounded.

Rituals are difficult to add to a Family Culture and old patterns or ritual behaviors are equally as difficult to extinguish. It takes great commitment and resolve.

The Walsh Family arrived on time for their Family Meeting at my office two weeks later. I had heard from the boys twice via email with questions about their Family Constitution.

"So, who wants to lead the Family Meeting?" I asked.

"I will for today, but Rose and I discussed having the four of us rotate who was going to lead the meeting," Steven replied.

"Great . . . go for it Steven." I said with a smile.

"Okay, I think the best way to get started is to apologize to you boys for how we were trying to communicate with you. We felt we had to keep pushing you to keep you at the level you are at. We didn't think about that you needed to learn to be there yourself. We also want to hear about the Family Constitution and then go around and see what each of you need from us," Steven said proudly.

Side note . . . I didn't ask Mr. Walsh to attend to the feelings of his sons as he opened the Family Meeting. When you organize the "content" of your life with ritual and structure, you begin to experience the intention of your own feelings. The Walshs' intention to coach their children was being altered by the fear that the boys would fail . . . even though they never had before.

"Wow . . . that's awesome, Dad. Here is what we came up with, with some help from Dr. D.," Stevey said, also beaming proudly.

The family went through all the points on the Family Constitution and the parents were just amazed at how thoroughly their sons knew what was expected of them and what would happen if they didn't follow the rules. Everyone had a chance to speak and everyone delivered themselves respectfully and with kindness.

The Family Meeting became a ritual that every member of the Walsh family embraced and identified with. When you embrace something new and make it a ritual that you identify with, it makes it much easier to consistently carry on.

Rituals do help create identity.

The Family Meeting is a ritual that provides a safe place for family members to review each week, the set of rules, expectations and schedules for upcoming events. It allows parents to attend to their feelings about the standard they have for their children and address them consistently without the disrespect of constantly "badgering."

It also allows the child to learn to self-regulate within the family culture while consistently receiving the coaching and guidance necessary, but without the need to react disrespectfully to their parents.

RITUALIZED TIME WITH YOUR CHILD.

When I was a little boy, every Saturday afternoon, my father and I would take his Oldsmobile Delta 88 to the local automated car wash. (This was a big deal back then. The automated car wash was a brand new invention where you could actually drive your car onto a track that would pull you through the car wash while you stayed in your car and watched the process unfold. It was awesome!)

All week long, no matter what went on, I remember looking forward to that time of the week when my father and I (without my brother tagging along) would get into the car, drive to the car wash and perform our weekly ritual. It was OUR thing to do! It was part of our identity together. I am sure my father and my brother had their own thing, but the weekly car wash was ours.

My mother and I had "ritualized time" together as well. Although not intended to be ritualized time together, our regular trips to all the doctors for my scoliosis issues became just that, ritualized time together that I look back on with great love and fondness.

You see, my mother didn't drive a car back then, so to get to all the appointments, we would have to wait at the bus stop, take the bus to the Skokie Swift, the train that connected our suburb to the city, wait for the Skokie Swift, take it to the Howard "El," the train that took us to downtown Chicago, then walk from the train to the doctor's office.

The commitment my mother made to get me the medical help I needed was profound. Although I dreaded what happened at the doctor's office (all that twisting, turning, poking and prodding,) I always looked forward to the journey to the doctor's office with my mom.

Our journey, with all its sights, sounds and smells was just that, OURS . . . my mom's and mine. I have etched memories of the RITUALIZED TIME spent with each of my parents that both define my relationship with each of them growing up, and helped me to become the person I am today.

The intimacy of reciprocal interaction between my parents and me in a safe paradigm allowed me to express my voice and receive feedback while having the privacy and protection of the alone time together.

The beautiful thing about this time being ritualized for me was the wonderful anticipation of having the time with them again.

My rituals did help create my identity, and **RITUALIZED TIME between parent and child helps create the identity of the parent/child relationship as well as the individual, themselves.**

Parenting models speak to the concept of "quality time" between parent and child. Everyone agrees that "quality time" is a wonderful idea, but many parents struggle with creating the time or the "quality," let alone ritualizing it so that it becomes a consistent part of the culture and seen as a priority by the child.

Parents must see the value in spending one-on-one time with their child, regardless how busy they are or how many children they have in their family.

Here's a *great* story, about a *great* kid, from a *great* family . . .

The Harley's are a very large family. Dr. and Mrs. Harley have NINE children, ranging from age three to 19-years-old.

Dr. John Harley is a cardiologist in private practice and works all the time. Eileen Harley is a stay at home mom, who, frankly, will joke that it seems as if she has been pregnant longer than the time she hasn't.

The Harley's are devout Catholics which accounts for the many pregnancies.

I met the Harley's when their middle daughter, Melissa (they actually have three sets of middle daughters and she is from the first grouping,) asked to speak to a therapist.

Melissa, 15-years-old, sat in my office and if I had closed my eyes, I would have sworn that I was talking to a 30-year-old woman. That is what sometimes happens in these large families when the older kids are asked to help out with the younger kids, they mature very quickly.

I was expecting to hear how much she hates living in a large family, or which sibling or parent she has a problem with. But to my surprise, Melissa was worried about her parents.

"I worry for my parents all the time," she opened with.

"Do you worry about their relationship with one another? Are they fighting all the time?" I asked.

"Oh no, nothing like that. I worry that with all 11 of us to take care of, they work all the time and never have time with anyone," she explained.

"Have you shared your concerns with them?" I pursued.

"Sure, but they tell me that there just isn't time for any of that. My dad needs to work and his patients need him and my mom has meals, laundry, diapers (still), homework and everything to do for all of us," she said.

"Sounds exhausting," I mused.

"It's awesome, really. I am so proud of my family. We all get along, help out and take care of each other. I just want some time with each of them and so do my siblings," she finished explaining.

Melissa was looking for "ritualized time" with her parents. She knew she had a need for that special, "quality time" with each of her parents to identify herself beyond the family culture experience she was living in. She knew that there was an important piece missing.

"Maybe we should ask your parents to join us and brain storm the best way to approach the feasibility of this?" I suggested.

"Great. I will ask them to call you," she said as if she got the deal she came for.

The Harley Family is quite remarkable. They already had a Family

Constitution in place, with Family Meetings set up weekly to keep order and consistency in the Family Culture.

John and Eileen Harley somehow knew to "respond without judgment" and not "react" to their children. And whether it was by design, or necessity of the shear number of children in the household, they were already on the "sidelines" of their children's experiences and the children were experiencing the intentions of their feelings and self regulating.

Thus, Melissa at age 15 knew how she felt, had a voice around those feelings and was ready to figure out if she can get what she felt she needed.

I introduced myself again to the Harleys, whom I met briefly prior to Melissa's appointment.

"Melissa explained to us why she wanted to see someone. We support her in this effort but we don't know how to resolve this for her. We have literally no more room in the schedule for anything new, let alone one on one time with each of the kids," John opened up with.

"I want to thank you for coming in to meet with us. I know you are busy people. Melissa's request seems ambitious to say the least," I replied.

"Are you saying that this is impossible to pull off?" Melissa directed at me.

"Oh, no, not at all. I just want your parents to understand the intention of your feelings and not focus on how overwhelming it might feel to add one more thing to their list." I explained.

"How do you feel, Melissa?" Eileen asked quietly.

"I'm missing something. I am so afraid that I will grow up and have no memories of special times I shared with each one of you. I know some of the others feel the same way," Melissa shared with tears streaming down her cheek.

"Melissa's intuition about 'ritualized time' with her parents is right on. However, it doesn't have to be as frequent as she might think. Maybe we can come up with a schedule that would give her what she needs without overwhelming you guys anymore than you are?" I suggested.

"Well, if we do this for her, everyone else is going to want in on this and that's just too much," Eileen said with John shaking his head in agreement.

"Let's try this in reverse as if you had only one child, rather than nine," I suggested.

"What do you mean, Phil?" John asked.

"If you were to set up one ritual with one child, what would it be?" I asked.

"I know!" Blurted out Melissa.

"Okay, tell us what you think, Melissa." Her father replied.

"If I was an only child, I would just want one meal alone with you, just the two of us. Breakfast or lunch. Something like that, just to talk," she said.

"So, John and Eileen, if there was a time each week when you could have a meal with one child alone, when would that be?" I continued with that line of thinking.

"That's so tough because there is not just one." Eileen said in defeat.

"Well, no there ARE nine children, but there IS just one of you. So let's create a time when you can have a meal with one child and the nine children will rotate through week after week. If both you and John find that one time you can commit to each week, your children will get 'ritualized time' with each parent, roughly every four and a half weeks," I tried to explain slowly. (We are going to need a calculator for this one, you know?)

"That's a fabulous idea! I love it! Hey every four weeks or so is way better than nothing. Can we try this Mom and Dad?" Melissa blurted out.

"Okay, I guess so. I guess I can do breakfast early on Saturdays if everyone is willing to get up early when I am on-call. How about you Mom?" John asked with a calm resolution.

"I guess I can take each one of you for a quick dinner on Tuesdays when your Dad comes home early," Eileen replied with fatigue in her voice.

"Thank you Mom and Dad. Thank you so much for trying this. Let's go in order from youngest to oldest because the young ones won't want to wait to get started," Melissa suggested with great enthusiasm.

"Awesome. I am so happy we found a way to solve this for Melissa without overwhelming you guys too much. Now, rituals are really hard to keep up, especially when the culture is already so patterned and busy. I want you to try it for nine weeks without exception and then we can meet to see if it is meeting your needs," I concluded.

Nine weeks went by quickly and Melissa came back with her parents.

The ritual was firmly in place and the children were each getting "ritualized time" with each one of their parents. Melissa said it best in this follow-up meeting.

She said, "I know it's not a lot of time with my parents, but at least now I feel like I am going to get to know them as people and they are going to get to know me."

. . . I told you this was a *great* story, about a *great* kid, from a *great* family!

CHAPTER NINE

Parenting as a Basketball Metaphor

Parents must teach, guide, coach, and love their child through their child's experience. Parents must respond rather than react to preserve their child's safety to feel the intention of their moment. Parents create a Family Culture that embraces their values, standards and expectations that identify them as individuals and as a family. Parents need a structure and a set of rules and consequences that help govern the family members while allowing each of them to navigate freely in the culture in which they live.

And of course, from all of this, the GOAL is for the child to grow up able to self-regulate, living freely to make their own choices, with a fully developed sense of self and others.

PARENTS . . . We can build the Family Culture. We can learn to let it be the child's own experience. We can learn to respond and not react. We can set the structure, rules and consequences. And now, we must teach our children the skills necessary to self-regulate effectively. (Remember, it's still their choice to use those skills you teach them, right?)

It's time for a BASKETBALL METAPHOR . . . I would imagine that you understand enough about the game of basketball to know that there are two baskets set on posts that are ten feet high; one at each end of a court.

The goal for one team is to move that ball toward their designated end of the court, shoot the ball into their basket and win points when the ball makes it through the basket rim.

The goal of the other team is to DEFEND the basket, and find a way NOT to let the other team be successful when they shooting the basketball into the net.

Of course, there is a STRUCTURE to the court and a SET OF RULES for both teams as they navigate themselves in the game and on the basketball court. Under the rules of basketball, a player is only allowed to touch the ball, and NOT touch the player who has the ball.

Another important rule for our purposes is that the player, who HAS the ball, must "dribble" the ball, (bounce it) only within the boundaries of the court in order to advance themselves to their designated basket.

METAPHORICALLY . . . The basketball court is the space (Family Culture and Structure) given by the parent for the child to experience their moment . . . to dribble their ball. The child is the player "dribbling" the ball toward their designated basket. The basketball, itself, is the child experiencing their moment, filled with all the expectations and rules of the Family Culture and Structure.

The Parent is the COACH of the player needing to learn the skills of the game.

As a coach, parents must teach the rules of the game, how to handle the ball, and the strategies of how to navigate the ball down the court.

An effective coach knows when to get on the practice court and work with their player on a few moves, and when to step onto the sideline of the court and let the player play.

There are two types of DEFENSE in the game of basketball . . .

1. "MAN-TO-MAN" is one strategy for the player defending the basket from the player with the ball. Wherever the player with the ball dribbles, the defender is right there with them. When the ball handler moves left, the defender moves left with them. When the ball handler moves right, the defender is sure to be right in step with them. Why? . . . To make sure you guide the ball handler where YOU want them to move, not necessarily where THEY want to move.

The only rule, (and risk) with this strategy is that you cannot interfere with the ball handler's dribbling of the ball. You cannot touch the player with the ball at all, or it is considered a penalty. And that can be tricky, because when you are "man-to-man," you can be right on top of the player with the ball.

2. "ZONE" is also a strategy for the player defending the basket from the player dribbling their ball.

This strategy has the defender backing up a little and giving the ball handler a "zone" to freely dribble in. As long as the ball handler dribbles inside the zone you are giving them, they are left alone to dribble.

If the ball handler tries to push through the zone to get to their designated basket, the defender then moves close up, intervenes, and guides them back to the zone where the ball handler is allowed to dribble freely.

The Zone defense can be a very effective strategy when the ball handler is a skilled dribbler. Why? Because you don't want to get yourself in a "power struggle" with a skilled player and risk that the ball handler will find a way to get around you on their way to their basket.

You want to honor their ball handling skills and give them a space ("zone") to dribble, without giving them the full court to shoot the ball.

As I said earlier, effective coaches know when to get on the practice court with their player and teach the skills of the game, and they know when to step to the sideline of the court and let the player play.

When it is "practice time," coaches need to have a strategy of how they are going to teach the skills required to play the game effectively.

Parenting is the coaching of a fluid strategy that transitions from "man-to-man" to "zone" based on the skill level of the child! The goal is to ready your child to "dribble" their ball in the largest zone possible . . . the basketball court of their own life!

STRATEGY FROM BIRTH TO 10-YEARS-OLD.

Please remember that every child learning the game of life matures at their own rate, and these age boundaries are rough estimates based on the developmental readiness of where children seem to be at that age.

From birth to age 10, the parent (coach,) should consider primarily the defensive strategy of "MAN-TO-MAN."

Young children require the "hands on" practice while their coach is following their ball handling every step of the way. Think about it . . . Babies need "man-to-man" coaching to be given the necessary basics to survive and grow. The parent is focused on their safety and their needs, and have no thought of backing off their child's experience.

A 2-year-old needs the "man-to-man" coaching as they practice what is safe to touch, what is dangerous and what are basic appropriate behavioral skills.

When parents bring their young child with them into my office (which is not "child proofed" for little ones,) they are constantly needing to get up and guide "junior" away from the electrical socket or the piece of artwork that is sitting on top of my bookcase. Wherever the child goes, the parent goes. (Or I go, when I have parents inexplicably sitting there, letting their child touch whatever they want. Maybe they are in a different kind of a zone, as in completely "zoned out!")

A 4-year-old needs the "man-to-man" coaching as they practice what is safe, how to communicate, and how to socialize. Parents are right there with their 4-year-old, teaching and guiding their child with the values, rules and structure required of the culture.

Parents begin to incorporate a little "zone" in their child's practice, with playgroups and preschool experiences, while understanding that they must go "man-to-man" as the child practices the skills of making choices within those environments.

A 6-year-old needs "man-to-man" coaching about the set of rules and consequences of the Family Culture and their School Culture as they are learning to incorporate their own decision making skills into various cultures that they are regularly a part of.

As you can see, though, there is even more need and readiness for some "zone" defense in this age group's practice. Parents must be ready to move in and out of these two defenses with this age group, understanding that they still need more "man-to-man" than "zone."

Ages eight through 10-year-olds need less "man-to-man" coaching as they have frequently been in "zone" environments by now, with expectations that they are close to having the skills necessary to navigate on their own.

Parents are very active in moving in and out of the two strategies, understanding that the child is again needing more "zone" to practice as they increase their skill set. This age group requires parents to understand well the skill level of their particular child, so that they don't move them into too large of a "zone" when the child still needs "man-to-man" practice with their coach. This can be a tricky time for parents.

If a child is well skilled, even at 8"years-old, they will begin to push the boundaries of the practice. Parents must be willing to let the child try, under the supervision of their coach, only to pull back into "man-to-man" when necessary.

STRATEGY FOR AGES 10 THROUGH 18-YEARS-OLD.

The "Zone" defense approach for parents, as they assist their child on the practice court, is the strategy of choice for children who are merging out of childhood (pre-teens) and into adolescence (teenagers,) as well as adolescence to adulthood, of course.

By this time, the player with the ball (your child with their own experience) believes they have the skills necessary to dribble their ball to the basket; to take their experience where they want it to go. The coach MUST remain in open and honest communication with this age group (easier said than done, by the way) to make sure there is a realistic assessment of their level of skill and a true readiness to dribble their ball alone on the basketball court of life.

Between ages 10 and 18, the skill level of dribbling the ball (managing their own experience) will improve dramatically, if the parent continues to increase the space of the "zone" and reduce the frequency of "man-to-man" as the child's readiness dictates.

This age group is not able to practice on the court totally alone and still requires the coaching necessary for effective ball handling. (On some level, children of all ages may require some practice time with their coach, don't you think? The role of coach may change in your life as an adult, but the need for coaching is always there. (That is something that I personally experience all of the time.)

Parents must be available to practice on the practice court with their child, and not assume they can do this alone. However, they also must to be ready to step on the sideline of the court, letting their child practice and play in their own game.

This age group requires plenty of practice time in a "zone" defense with their coach, learning the advanced skill of decision making on the court with all the boundaries of the "zone" firmly in place, just in case the child dribbles too close to the edge of the "zone."

SO . . . as a child grows up, they will need their parent to coach them on the practice court of their life. While children are young they need a hands on, "man-to-man" approach to learn the game rules and begin their ball handling skills.

As they get older, the ball handlers are increasingly put into "zone" situations in their lives, so they are going to need more practice with their coach in a "zone" practice situation. (Makes sense? I hope so!)

The secret to effective coaching (and thus, effective parenting,) then is to understand when your child needs "man-to-man" practice and when they are ready to practice in a "zone."

How will you know when your child needs one over the other? The answer is simple . . . Your child will tell you through the truth of their experience and their intention to feel their moment. You will hear them loud and clear if you are "responding" and not "reacting" to them in judgment.

Regardless of "everyone else's" agenda or the "picture" of what "ought to be," you, as their parent (coach) must live in the truth of your child and guide them to know when they are skillful enough to dribble on their own and self-regulate on the court of their life.

If you keep them "man-to-man" while their ball handling skills require more space to maneuver, you will risk the "power struggle" that results and the child's attempt to get around you and beat you to the basket.

Remember . . . "Going Underground?" Parents never want to be put into that situation with their child. Yet, it seems so common with families of adolescents today. Parents lose their effectiveness as their child's coach. Also, children should never be forced into that "power struggle" situation because they will feel the pressure to go around their parent and may not be ready to take on the whole court, alone.

Parents just have to be ready to give their child the chance to practice with more space. Let them practice without fear that while they are dribbling, they may "draw" that dreaded "foul." ("Drawing a foul" is the metaphor for failure or making a mistake.)

Drawing a foul, making a mistake, or failing to advance the ball IS NOT the end of the game! Mistakes and failure in the game of life only means the player needs MORE practice, right? It cannot be "success at all cost," anymore! It's just a moment that perhaps requires more coaching! If your child draws a foul, you as their coach must willing to go back onto the practice court (without reaction and judgment) and show them a few moves that might help. You teach, guide, coach and love them, without taking the ball away from them, because of your own fear of the "foul." It's still their game you are coaching!

Let me tell you a story about Mary Crawford . . .

Mary Crawford is the youngest of two in the Crawford family. Mary is currently 18-years-old. She has a brother, Daniel, who is just 4-years-old and is now living in New York, after graduating from University of Illinois.

Jason and Hilary Crawford worked very hard to create the family culture they wanted for Daniel and Mary. They have the perfect house, in the perfect neighborhood, in the perfect school district.

Mary and Daniel attended all the community functions that their parents believed were important. They were involved in everything they thought was necessary to belong to their community.

The Crawfords follow the "what everyone else is doing" theory of Family Culture, which prescribes for them what the appropriate thing to do and have is for their "picture" for their family.

Daniel seemed to always fit that "picture" with his truth quite nicely. Everything came easy for him and he was the model of "what everyone else" was doing. He was always popular, a great athlete and was invited to all the "in crowd" social gatherings. He was even accepted to the complete list of colleges that the "community" deemed appropriate to attend.

Mary, on the other hand, has never quite fit the "picture" her parents wanted for her, regardless how hard she tried. She was not a popular girl in the community growing up and only participated in all the social gathering under duress. She was accepted into only one of the appropriate colleges and her parents demanded she attend.

Mary was truly never allowed to get on the "practice court" of her own experience, let alone have a voice in the practice of the game she was being forced to play.

Jason and Hilary Crawford knew how to coach "man-to-man" well and did so with both kids when they were young. As Daniel got older, the Crawfords felt comfortable moving into a "zone" for him as appropriate.

With Mary, the Crawfords never felt comfortable moving out of "man-to-man" and into a "zone" to allow her space to dribble on her own. As Mary grew up, the more her parents practiced with her, the more frustrated they all became. Mary never quite embraced the skills of the game the Crawfords believed were so important for their Family identity. Subsequently, Mary was never given her space (a "zone") to practice her own ball handling (managing her own experience) in a game she would choose.

Mary didn't fit their "picture" and the Crawfords were going to stay on the court with her until she did, regardless of her age. (By the way, this is a very unfortunate and common dynamic in families today. So, please remember what I have been telling you . . . it's your child's experience, not yours. We cannot force our children to be someone they are not, just because we have our "picture" for them.)

Mary lived in a community growing up where "every girl" wore a size two and got straight A's. (Really . . . "every girl?" Come on now!) This was, however the very picture of "everyone else" that her parents believed in for her. There was just one thing wrong with their picture of Mary . . . Mary Crawford was obese and she struggled to get C's and B's in school. Mary COULD NOT and eventually WOULD NOT try anything more to learn the skills they were demanding.

The Crawfords took her to every tutor and service out there to help with her grades. They dragged her to weight loss camps and clinics ever since she was 3-years-old. Mary had been to eight different therapists before coming to me!

Mary's parents kept her in a "man-to-man" strategy throughout her life growing up. She was so buried in her parents efforts to force her into being "everyone else" that she lost all clarity of her own self. She was never allowed a space to practice the skills that best represented her truth and the intentions of her feelings.

Mary couldn't do anything on her own without some form of "man-to-man" scrutiny. It stopped being coaching long ago. Every behavior, every food, every homework assignment, every single thing was scrutinized by the Crawfords.

Mary didn't know what to do, except try to please her parents "above ground" and go "underground" with her feelings and her choices behind their back.

Mary went to all the functions her parents wanted her to go to, but didn't talk to anybody while she was there.

Mary followed every diet, in front of her parents, but had snacks hiding under her bed and in her locker.

Mary tried hard at home with her schoolwork, but at school, would often skip class and smoke cigarettes behind the school building.

Yes, Mary, even graduated and went off to the one college "everyone" goes to; the one that her parents picked for her. (Lucky for the Crawfords, because it was the only one of the "permissible" colleges she was accepted to.)

You see the Crawfords had the "take your daughter to college" experience like "everyone else" but, guess what? Mary lasted three weeks there. She didn't speak to anyone, didn't go to class, and didn't have the skills to navigate her own experience.

Mary Crawford was lost!

She had no decision making skills to navigate her own experience. She called her mother 10 to 12 times a day, needing her "man-to-man" guidance on her cell phone. She had never had the opportunity to find her own "game" and get enough "zone" practice to know how to self-regulate.

Mary was in crisis and needed to come home. The Crawfords were embarrassed and ashamed of Mary. The truth is they have always been embarrassed and ashamed of Mary.

Side note . . . Please don't get me wrong here. The Crawfords love their daughter very much. They truly believed that what was best for Mary was to be like the community of people THEY felt most comfortable with. The difficulty here is that the Crawfords' agenda was NOT Mary's truth and the judgment of that kept the Crawfords from embracing Mary.

Jason and Hilary Crawford knew they could not avoid what was happening with Mary. They drove to her college three weeks after they brought her to new student week, picked up Mary with all her things and brought her home.

Mary sat in my office, crying, as her mother yelled at her for embarrassing the family all these years.

"What are you going to do now? What do you want me to tell "everyone"? Why can't you be normal like "everyone else?" She yelled.

"Okay Mrs. Crawford. We get your point. I think we need to go a different direction here. Yelling at your daughter just isn't going to help us. I can't tell you what to do at home, but in my office, you aren't going to condemn her for this. It just isn't productive." I said forcefully.

Mary started crying uncontrollably, as if every feeling and emotion that was built up inside of her was finally gushing out.

"Mrs. Crawford, would it be okay with you if I spend a little time with Mary alone and then we can bring you back in, in just a few minutes?" I asked.

Mrs. Crawford got up and went into the waiting room without saying a word.

As soon as I escorted Mary's mother out of the door, I sat back down, and Mary stopped gushing.

"I am so sick of her judging me." Mary said, her sobs slowing down to a quiver.

"You're so fat! Everyone stares at you! Why can't you just fit in? You are not normal!" Mary said in a voice mocking her mother.

"I'm sorry. It sounds so painful for you," I said in a soothing tone.

Side note . . . It was so hard for me to handle myself in that moment. I can feel Mary's pain. My father lived in pictures too. I grew up hearing him tell me to "sit up straight, people are staring at you." I couldn't sit up straight, my spine was curved like an "S," for God's sake! I didn't tell Mary any of that. It would not have been very professional of me. But it was tough stuff for me to hear.

Back to Mary . . . "What am I going to do? I can't go back there. I don't want to be around any of those people!" She yelled.

"We are going to slow all this down and let your parents know that you are home for now and that you are going to work in here with me to figure out YOUR life plan . . . at least the next step. Okay?" I reassured her.

"Okay. But do I have to be in here when you tell her?" She asked in a panic.

"Of course you do. You are the one who is going to tell her," I said with a grin.

Mary's mother walked back into the room. She started talking before she even sat back down.

"Mary, why don't you just stay home for the semester, work with Phil in here, and figure out what you need to do to get a grip," Hilary said in her judgmental but "trying to be kind" kind of way.

Mary was ready to react but I intervened.

"You know Mrs. Crawford, we came to the same conclusion in here. Great minds do think alike. I agree with your plan, with one caveat." I said abruptly.

"What's that? She asked.

"If we find that there is a better, healthier plan for Mary other than going back to that school, will you embrace it?" I asked.

"Yes, but it has to be something Mr. Crawford and I agree to," she declared looking at Mary.

"Of course, you are Mary's parents. Of course!" I concluded.

Mary didn't have to tell her mother anything, after all. (Boy, I have to help this kid get a voice!)

"Mary, what kind of schedule are you living with these days so we can make our appointment?" I asked jokingly.

Everyone started laughing, needing some comic relief.

Mary came alone for her next visit with me.

"What's new Mary? I asked.

"My dad won't even talk to me and my mom told her friends that I have mononucleosis," she said angrily.

"'Mono' is a permissible explanation to save face with her community. Right?" I asked.

"Of course, but why doesn't she just tell the truth? That I am a fat loser and couldn't cut it!" She blurted out.

"Is that the truth for you? Do you believe what they all believe?" I continued asking.

"They're my parents and this is all I ever heard my whole life. What else should I believe?" She challenged.

"Mary, if you believed the 'script' that your parents and the community had for you, you wouldn't be in conflict. You would be sitting in class right now back at school," I said.

"What do you mean?" she asked, perking up a little.

"Well, follow me here for awhile . . . People are only in crisis or conflict when change is necessary. Otherwise we would be comfortable even in our discomfort of the paradigm we are in. You are not and have never been comfortable in your discomfort. You are miserable in this paradigm. For example, if you were comfortable in the 'picture' everyone has for you, it would be YOUR truth, which means you would follow a diet and be as thin as you can be. You would be in school with all those kids your parents want you to be friends with. And you would not have to hide who you are from anyone. And you certainly would not be sitting in here with me when 'everyone else' is back at school. Does that make sense to you?" I presented looking for clarity and truth from Mary.

"I guess I follow you. You're saying . . . I wouldn't be miserable if I agreed with my parents opinion of me, so I must not agree with them," she said, so much more concisely than me. (Ahh . . . out of the mouths of babes).

"Exactly! Which means, our goal is to find out what you believe, not in reaction to them, but your own truth," I said with excitement. (I love this stuff!)

"So how do we do that?" She asked exhaustedly.

"Well, I have homework for you for the next time we meet. I need you to bring in picture albums from when you were in elementary school through high school. In the meantime, I would like to meet with your parents next if that's okay? I promise to keep our conversations confidential. I just need to teach them to back off from you a bit," (zone) I explained.

"Sure, but good luck with that!" she said rolling her eyes.

The next time they came in to see me, Jason and Hilary Crawford sat in silence in my office waiting for a report from me.

"It's been a painful, scary time for you guys." I said opening the dialogue.

"We knew deep down that she would fail. She has never lived like everybody else. We just failed as parents." Hilary said with tears streaming down her cheek.

(Educable moment here folks . . . Truth without judgment is essential for a healthy relationship with your child and for teaching them to self-regulate. Do you guys hear the judgment in Hilary's comments and that she is more focused on her agenda of her success than Mary's truth? Hilary "reacts" and doesn't "respond" and is so far away from Mary's feelings.)

"I need your help to help Mary." I said, ignoring all the judgment she had just spewed.

"What can we do to fix this?" asked Jason, Mary's father.

"Well, I know that Mary has been quite a disappointment to you. The truth is she won't be able to meet the expectations you have for her. She knows that and you know that. You just have to accept that, without condemning her for it. The real crisis for Mary right now, is that she is 18-years old and has no confidence and no life skills to operate out there in the world on her own without you. We need to set up something while she is home with you to teach her the skills she needs. She may never be that girl in the community you wanted, but right now, she won't be in *any* community. She will be living in your basement for the foreseeable future. At the very least, you will be on the phone with her throughout her life . . . coaching her through every step she takes," I said, boldly.

"You are so sure of yourself. That's a lot to swallow. What do you mean, she won't be able to meet our expectations?" Hilary pounced all over me.

"Mary has never been able to be the thin girl you wanted her to be, or the socialite her brother is, or the student you hoped for," I began to elaborate.

Hilary interrupted me with . . . "I don't accept that. What's going to happen to her if she doesn't learn to live like 'everyone else?' She is not going to live in our basement for the rest of MY life. Over my dead body!"

"Exactly, Mrs. Crawford. Let me explain my thoughts about Mary and frankly all kids growing up today. You guys love your daughter so much and want the best for her. Of course. You have given her all the tools and coaching to get her to where you think she should be. Okay. But that's not where she is at. So we start where the truth is, not where we think it 'ought to be.' I am sorry for that, but this is exactly where she is at. It's time to take an approach that gives Mary a voice in her own experience. It's time that we let Mary dictate the pace of the game. In order to do that, we need you to trust that she will get to where she is comfortable living her life, independent of you. It will be your choice as to whether you are proud of who she becomes; who she really has always been," I tried to explain without any more interruptions.

"Okay, I get it. So what do you want from us?" Jason asked.

"I want you to let Mary live at home, get a part time job of some kind to be somewhat productive and work on her goals. I need you to teach and guide her to do things on her own, whatever it may be. She needs you to coach her without judging her. And she needs time to practice," I said summing this up.

"Well, what about school?" Jason asked.

"I don't know. Let's see what Mary comes up with," I replied.

"We don't really have much choice here do we? She has always resisted what we expected from her," Hilary concluded.

"We don't have a choice in who our children see themselves to be. Our job is to help them to be the best they can be in WHO THEY ARE and hope they learn to self-regulate out there in the world. It's ultimately their choice to make; it's their life to live. We already made our choice," I said elaborating on Hilary's point.

"You can lead a horse to water, but you can't make it drink," Jason followed.

"EXACTLY! And we have to stop blaming them for not being thirsty!" I finished with.

Mary Crawford found a part time job at a preschool near her house.

She visited with me regularly, focusing on the pictures from her past (literally and figuratively.)

It was clear to her (and to me) that she had to tackle the "fat and ugly" script that she was taught to believe.

"Phil, can I ask you a question?" Mary asked.

"Sure Mary, anything. You know that," I replied.

"I don't mean to hurt your feelings but . . . how did you deal with looking so weird growing up?" She asked with a frightened look on her face.

"Great question, Mary. You know, when I was about your age, I finally dealt with the name calling by kids in my class, let alone the message my father had pummeled me with. You see, I knew what he thought and I knew that people stared, but I never truly thought I looked different. It comes down to your own truth, your own feelings about it, not everyone else's," I explained.

"Isn't that just so hard to do?" She asked.

"Yes . . . and no! Yes, because there was so much of that message around me that maybe if they all felt that way about me, then perhaps I am that way. But no . . . No, because if I really don't believe what they believe, why is their opinion of me greater than my own? Isn't my voice . . . my truth . . . wait . . . more importantly . . . Isn't YOUR voice, YOUR truth equally as important as anyone else's, even your own parents?" I said from the deepest place in my heart.

"That's what I'm figuring out. My parents have been pretty good lately. They are letting me do things that they never let me do before. My mom taught me how to do my laundry and I asked her to take me to her gym and teach me to exercise. Hey, wait . . . what happened when you were my age that you figured this out for yourself?" She asked.

"I'm so glad that your parents are giving you some space and time to learn some things you need to know and to try out some things like exercising.

"Oh . . . well, it was Spring Break, my freshman year of college, and a group of my new friends went to Daytona Beach, Florida. (Daytona Beach was the 'in place' to go for Spring Break back in the mid 70s!)

We arrived at our hotel, everyone put their swimsuits on and we ran down to the beach. I realized when I made it down to the beach that I always wore a tee shirt with my swim trunks because I didn't want people to see my 'crooked body' and stare at me. It was my 'moment of truth' right there and then. I wasn't my parents' little boy anymore and now I had to decide if I was going to live my life hiding who I was. It was my life to live and I had to decide if I believed what they all believed," I explained.

"So what did you do?" Mary asked, mesmerized by the story.

"I did what I had to do to set myself free. With tears streaming down my face, I pulled off my shirt for the entire world to see me! And you know what? No one looked, no one cared, no one laughed, and no one stared!" I said, with tears again welling up in my eyes.

"Wow, I am so ready to do that too, Phil . . . really!" Mary said as we both cried together.

"I know Mary. I could tell and I am so proud of who you are," I said reaching out to hold her hand.

Jason and Hilary Crawford moved from a "man-to-man" to a "zone" while Mary lived at home again. They gave Mary space and time to figure out her own game and the court she was going to play on.

It was not easy for either of them to face their community with the truth. They, like me on the beach in Daytona, believed the world would stare and judge.

But for Mary, she embraced their coaching, tried out different "courts" to practice on, and found her voice and her truth along the way.

Today, Mary Crawford works full time as a hostess at a very fancy restaurant in a very cool area of the city. She lives with her boyfriend in an apartment three blocks from work. She has her own social life from her restaurant world. She has no plans to return to school.

A beautiful side note . . . Mary lost 85 pounds since I began meeting with her. Funny, though, we never spoke once about a plan to lose weight. She just made it apart of her truth.

CHAPTER TEN

Teach, Guide, Coach, Love

FROM ONE PARENT TO ANOTHER.

O ur world has become a scary place to raise a child. More and more people say to me they are not sure that they want to bring a child into this world. As parents, I hope we would all agree that no matter how crazy and complicated this world has become, or will become in the future, the experience of raising a child, and the experience we have as children growing up in this world is well worth the effort.

Most of us reading this book are parents, but ALL of us reading this book are someone's child. It is up to each and every one of us to understand the culture we are creating and take the responsibility to make the changes necessary to shape our culture in a way that will allow for each individual child to grow emotionally, physically, completely, and develop into an independent adult who can self-regulate in the world around them.

We must understand what we are doing today that promotes and inhibits such an effort. Parents must understand what it takes to "raise a conscience as we raise a child."

The story of Brian Smith in Chapter One, tells of a teenage boy who is growing up trapped between the truth of who he is and the "picture" his parents had for him.

You remember, Brian Smith had no intention of being a student and should not have graduated high school, but his parents "brokered" a deal with the school to let him "walk" during his high school graduation. His parents got him through high school, got him into college and got the "picture" they needed.

Of course, once left to his own effort at college, Brian Smith was asked to leave. Brian Smith was not a student.

There was a truth about Brian Smith as there is a truth about all of us. His truth was so far removed from his experience, that it took living out on his own, struggling to make ends meet and coming back to his feelings of his moment to recognize that he wanted something different and he was going to have to take responsibility for his effort. Today, Brian Smith is an assistant head chef at a five-star hotel. Think of the level of judgment parents must have and the constant comparative analysis required in order to fit children into a picture that they actually don't fit in to.

Think what we must be doing to the self-esteem of our children when we give them a message that WHO they are is only good enough when it coincides with the picture we create for them.

Think what this must mean to the development of the child's psyche . . . the place where one's ethics, morals, character, and personality develop together to create one's identity . . . one's integrity . . . one's self-esteem.

We must change our attitude as parents and learn a different way. Our children are growing up in a world where the "picture" is definitely greater than the "truth."

We seem to have generation after generation of highly competent individuals growing up, knowing how to do many wonderful things I could never have imagined as a child. YET, we see more and more of these young people detached from the feelings of their moment and unable to self-regulate. We see more and more of these young people who clearly know right from wrong but don't really care. They seem to do whatever it is they wish to do for their own amusement regardless of who it hurts. (Remember the Rutgers University students and their practical joke that led to their friend's suicide?)

Parents have the responsibility to nurture the truth in their children without their own judgment becoming the agenda, so that their child can fully develop a clear sense of themselves, a clear sense of others, and a clear sense of their conscience. Being a parent is a daunting and overwhelming responsibility, although we are doing so many things right today as parents.

However, as we know so much more about parenting, we seem to be doing it with an attitude and in a culture that is just a step away from where it needs to be. We must get our parenting in-sync with our child's true conscience development.

RAISING A CONSCIENCE WHILE RAISING A CHILD.

In the 1950's Dr. Benjamin Spock was "the man" when it came to parenting in the post World War II era. His theory was groundbreaking as it focused on a brand new concept in raising children . . . the child's "self-esteem."

For Dr. Spock, children needed to feel "success" in order to feel good about themselves. The process of the experience, regardless of outcome, success or failure, was no longer as important as the particular outcome, itself.

Dr. Spock connected raising "healthy" children to successful outcomes and the praise and affirmation that the parents would give for that success. His model made perfect sense except that Dr. Spock could never have imagined that the world would "morph" into the competitive, "success at any and all cost" culture that it has become today.

It turns out that judging "failure" as a negative consequence and "success" as the only true valuable option has been FATAL to the complete development of a child's conscience and identity.

Avoidance of truthful moments, that are judged to be failure for the protection of a child's self-esteem, has proven to be central to the underdevelopment of the child's psyche. If an experience is judged to be a "failure" (negative) and considered non-permissible, **avoidance** of that failure becomes the goal and focus of the experience, **rather than** what you may actually feel or learn from that moment.

For many parents, the "picture of success" will override the "truth" of the authentic experience. We justify that by believing the truth of failure is too devastating to the child's self-esteem. BUT in reality, TRUTH of any kind is fundamental to the self-esteem of the child.

It's the JUDGMENT of that truth that puts the self-esteem at risk. And it's the voice of the parent who brings the judgment that gets in the way of the child's feeling of their experience.

Experiencing completely without interference by anyone else's judgment ALLOWS for one's own internal voice, one's psyche to process the experience. This creates a healthy, confident, truthful self!

Success and Failure, Judgment and Comparative Analysis, as a standard for self-esteem and identity are not only demotivating and diminishing to the child, they also do not allow the "self" to develop completely.

CONSCIENCE DEVELOPMENT . . . At birth, all children are universal. The whole human condition is an experience and an experience is the whole human condition. A baby's conscience, personality, value system, moral structure, are all one entity and one experience.

The first moment when behavior is no longer JUST an experience, but a PERFORMANCE to be evaluated and judged by someone else's view, is when a child begins to see themselves in COMPARISON to others. The child looks to the REACTION of the parent to make sense of themselves. They no longer feel the experience completely because they are now looking outside of the experience to determine whether someone else (parents) feel pleased or not with them.

You remember "Baby Sam," the son of the couple from my tennis group? Sam was an awesome baby, but you could see the anxiety and embarrassment (judgment) his parents had at his performing to their expectations at their party. Sam was being "Baby Sam" and that just wasn't good enough for his parents.

Every experience is filtered through one's psyche. The psyche is the "processing center" that blends our values, morals, intellect, personality and spirit into our identity. From that blending comes a process that allows us to view the world through our own interpretation.

THIS IS OUR CONSCIENCE.

Each person therefore has their own "True Personal World View," the way we see the world and the way we naturally choose to operate in the world we see. It isn't just our understanding of the "right and wrong" but our choice of how we represent ourselves and experience the decisions of what's "right or wrong."

There must be a way to teach our values, our preferences, and our culture to our children while protecting their psyche, their "processing center," and its development of their conscience.

If a child has a fully developed sense of self, without interference by someone else's judgment of the child's true personal world view, the child will be comfortable making choices based on their own experience.

EVERY MOMENT'S EXPERIENCE BEGINS WITH A FEELING.

This is how the true process of our experience goes . . .

FEELING. THOUGHT. DECISION. ACTION.

We feel the moment, create a thought from the feelings and make a decision to take action on our original feeling of the moment. When we create a thought from a feeling, that feeling combined with all of our past frames of reference relevant to the moment we are in, results in that thought and decision to take action.

The intention of the feeling, the reason "why" we are feeling what we are feeling in the moment creates the meaning of the experience and our identity.

IT IS OUR TRUTH!

If the agenda of someone else interferes with the experience we are having, we DETACH ourselves from the feeling of the moment and the thoughts we are having about those feelings. Our thoughts abandon the original feelings and attach themselves to DEFENDING against the judgment. We are forced to redirect to the feelings we have about the judgment in front of us.

Do you remember Molly Cook? Molly's story teaches us that no matter how much you try to put your parents' agenda in front of you as your own identity; your original feelings do not go away. They must be attended to, and your truth must be honored eventually.

Molly tried living life her parents' agenda. She dated who they wanted her to date. She lived where and how they expected her to live. She came close to marrying who they wanted her to marry. But in the end, she had to live her own truth, embracing her own true personal view of the world.

GOING UNDERGROUND.

"Success at all and any cost" brings with it the potential for dishonesty, for short cuts, for hiding one's truth and for "Going Underground."

Going Underground is that process of DETACHING from the feelings of the moment we are in (our truth) while ATTACHING our thoughts to whatever vigilance it takes to portray the "picture" of the agenda for our parents. It is disingenuous and illusionary.

Peter Robinson was the young man who went off to law school in Philadelphia, quit after his first semester and lived an illusion of being a law student until he was inadvertently caught by his parents. His story is large, shocking, and sad for sure.

But was I surprised at what a child will go through to keep the "picture" going, while avoiding the judgment, battle and consequences of his parents' reaction if he demanded to live his truth? Not at all.

For those who feel forced to create an illusion over their own truth, they live with a premise that is quite frightening . . . that they are NOT WORTHY of their own voice and that there is NO SPACE "ABOVE GROUND" for their truth, thoughts and decisions based on their own feelings.

Just think about a life experience where the standards by which we live and hold ourselves accountable to are communicated without judgment to our children, allowing them to live "above ground."

Just think of the possibilities if we are communicating in a way that supports and promotes the voice of our children while guiding their expectations with love and nurturance.

Just think if we lived in a culture that does not tolerate the "justifying" of the absence of integrity. The truth is, we as parents must find a way to communicate safely. Parents must encourage the voice of their child, and keep the family dynamics "above ground" by allowing for the feelings, thoughts and opinions of each family member to be welcome into the family culture.

PERFORMANCE.

Do you remember the story where Mrs. Betty Schwartz, Assistant Superintendent of Lizzy's school district asked her, "Are you ready to compete when you come to my school this fall?"

HUMAN BEINGS HAVE GONE FROM "HUMAN DOERS" TO "HUMAN PERFORMERS!"

Performance is so woven into our thinking that "winning" and "success" have become one in the same. Parents are taught today to build "success" as the ONLY permissible outcome. Performance is the standard that parents today have for their children. Performance is the "brush" that paints the "picture" parents have for their child in large part, because it is the "paintbrush" society has for all of us to utilize for our own success.

Today, parents believe that if "everyone else" is performing, then my child must perform too. Therefore, to compete and win, our children must keep up with "everyone else" or they will lag behind and have no chance for success . . . athletically, academically, and socially. That is the fear. That is the stress.

That is the culture we have chosen to accept. Here is the irony . . .

SUCCESSFUL PERFORMANCE
ACTUALLY REQUIRES NO JUDGMENT!

Society expects us to perform to win. THAT'S WRONG!

Our children today are parented to perform. THAT'S WRONG!

Performance today is judged completely by the outcome. THAT'S WRONG!

And parents are pushing their children all day long, frantically attempting to keep up with "everyone else." ABSOLUTLY WRONG!

Performance by definition is the process of "portraying" one's effort and intention to try. Performance must ONLY be about the intention to try, and the process of that effort, or we experience nothing, we feel nothing and we learn nothing about ourselves.

Sylvia Howard, our 80-year-old golfer experienced just that in her story. She could not allow herself to experience the feelings of her intention to try because of her judgment of her context.

In Sylvia's judgment, had Emily Swanson made it to the tournament, there would have been a very different outcome. (As if winning was everything and the experience of playing had little or no value!)

Sylvia's true experience in her performance was in her intention to try and her feeling of the moment, not the outcome of her score or the roster of players who attended. (Sylvia struggled with the judgment for failure even though she won!)

Inherent in the Theory of Performance is the foundation of "TRUTH WITHOUT JUDGMENT."

Don't you just love the story of Brad Bentley? His initial experience in the NFL was a rude awakening for him and it truly describes what we are talking about when we speak of performance theory.

Brad Bentley had all the talent in the world. But when failure became judgment, his performance went from the process of punting the ball to the judgment and avoidance of more failure.

No longer was Brad Bentley comfortable with himself. No longer was he feeling the moment of his process. No longer was he able to "portray his efforts" (perform) as he had countless times before in his career.

Performance on any stage in life requires a level of skill, discipline, consistency, practice, process and the acceptance of truth without judgment.

SUCCESS DOES NOT DEFINE SELF-ESTEEM.

Self-esteem is defined by one's effort and intention to try. Parents are the COACHES for their child's life. They provide the practice field, the rules of the game, the strategies, and the discipline to train, and also the love and support to keep practicing. BUT it is the child, who is the athlete of their own experience. It is the child who has to get out there on the practice field of life, practice and perform. Parents need to stay on the "sidelines" of the child's experience and coach.

Let's take a breath here for a moment . . . When I think of coaching our children to feel their OWN experience, I am reminded of a special song from my past. In the 1982 song, "Know Who You Are" by the band, "SuperTramp," the lyrics speak to the COURAGE one needs to listen to one's "voice." be guided by one's "heart" and be confident in knowing who you "truthfully" are! (I love the lyrics to this song and encourage each of you to seek them out. I used to sing them to my kids when they were little. Oy, you should hear me sing!)

Let's get back to what we have learned . . .

RESPONSIVE PARENTING
TRUTH WITHOUT JUDGMENT.

"Truth Without Judgment" refers to the "What is" rather than the "What should be" of an experience.

"What is the truth?" (fact) rather than "What should be the picture?"

Parents today have learned to parent their children based on the "picture" or agenda they have for their child rather than the child's actual experience. The parents' agenda seems, for the most part to be a combination of what they want for their child and what they feel "EVERYBODY ELSE" pictures for their children.

Judgment is the act of taking one's "preference" and "unsolicitely" assigning it to another person's circumstance, decision, choice or experience.

Every one of us has a "preference" about something BUT NO ONE really has a right to impose that preference onto someone else's experience unless requested. (That means our children as well!)

I am talking about OUR preference to control how a child should see the world, feel their experience and make choices based on our picture FOR them.

Our children MUST have a place to feel safe to succeed, to fail, to give effort, and to have feelings and an opinion about their own life's moment.

PARENTS MUST BE THAT PLACE FOR THEIR CHILD.

Parents . . . It is time to stop being fearful that your child is so different than "everybody else" and EMBRACE their individuality.

"RESPOND" TO YOUR CHILD, NEVER "REACT." Be a responsive parent to your child's experience.

"Reaction" is the expression of your feelings with your thoughts. (Emoting and Judging.)

"Response" is the expression of your thoughts about your feelings. (Process.)

Why "respond" rather than "react"? The safety created when communicating responsively allows for a parent to partner with their child. Through the partnership, a parent will be included in on a child's processing of their feelings that get interpreted into thoughts that become decisions and actions.

FEELING. THOUGHT. DECISION. ACTION.

This is the process of all experiences, and the development of identity comes from a child's intention to feel this process. Parents need to parent between FEELING and THOUGHT. (Where the true meaning of the experience lies.)

PROCESS RATHER THAN OUTCOME; INTENTION OF THE EXPERIENCE RATHER THAN CONTENT OF THE MOMENT.

Remember the story of my son, Justin and his decision to get a puppy? As a parent, I did not want him to get a puppy, certainly not while he was still in college. My agenda would have created a power struggle because Justin had an intention based on very strong feelings.

As a parent, I needed to respond between his feelings and his thoughts, not between his thoughts and his decision. He had already decided and there was nothing I could do, other than understand his feelings, be a safe place to share them, and coach, guide and educate him to a process that is going to be effective for him.

(By the way, his decision to get his dog has been a good one. Although he has had struggles financially to keep up with the pup, he is much less lonely and very responsible for the dog's care.)

RESPONSIVE PARENTING.

The other Justin story was when he was a little boy, and we were going to the toy store to buy his cousin a gift for Christmas. That was truly the birth of RESPONSIVE PARENTING.

I was no longer going to react to Justin's behavior when he didn't do what I asked him to do. I was going to try and see it through his intention.

What resulted in that experience is that I saw that if I held to the rules without reacting to his choices, he would ultimately have to take responsibility for his decisions, and I could be there to guide him through his feelings.

TRUST in yourself as your child's parent. Coaching, guiding, and educating your child with skills, information, and knowledge of your preferences will be impactful. You are the most influential person in your child's life for most of their growing up. Stay humble to that fact!

TRUST in yourself that you will remain the authority in their life even when you relinquish the power over them.

TRUST in your child. We all have feelings of intention in the moment of our experience and we have thoughts that make decisions to take an action. Your child is no different than we are in this human process. TRUST in the process with them and your child will feel confident on the voice of their own choices. After all, it is THEIR experience, NOT ours!

Do you remember the "Mohawk" story of Leslie Cochran and her sons, Matt and Jake?

Leslie Cochran is an awesome parent and had been working very hard at becoming a "responsive parent."

When Jake came home one day with a Mohawk haircut, she reacted to her agenda and didn't take into account Jake's intention of his feelings.

After taking pause and regrouping, she realized the need to be neutral, and to respond to what was going on for Jake. Leslie is that safe place for her sons and must remain conscious of that fact.

You do remember that it wasn't Leslie's reaction and power struggle that reached Jake? It was her responding to the intentions of his feelings; that he has never had a say in his own life. And it wasn't Leslie that influenced Jake to get rid of the Mohawk, it was the prettiest girl in his class!

FAMILY CULTURE.

Family Culture is a dynamic, living, breathing experience that protects, nurtures, and identifies the lives of the individuals who belong to it.

I shared with you the many memories that I have growing up that represent the identity of my family and me individually in that family culture. I shared with you the meaning of my mother's sweet and sour meatballs for the Jewish holiday. The sounds, smells and tastes that associate to that experience are so strong for me and truly represent moments that capture the essence of my family culture growing up.

Family Culture is the physical and emotional environment of the total experience of our family identity, growing up as a family member and as an individual.

FAMILY CULTURE CONSISTS OF FOUR R's . . . RULES, ROLES, RITUALS, and RELATIONSHIPS.

RULES . . . Every citizen has a right to live their life individually, independently and peacefully within the rules that govern them. Each culture is responsible to create and manage the set of rules necessary for the individual citizen to self-regulate and navigate within the culture.

ROLES . . . Family roles, like the family itself, must remain flexible and malleable to the circumstances facing the specific family culture at any given time in its development. The roles we take on and the response we receive for our approach to these roles, is critical to the functioning AND the identity of the individual in the family. A strong family identity comes from a strong sense of its roles as a family unit. And a strong individual identity comes from a strong sense of the individual's role in that family unit.

RITUALS . . . As a family culture lives with its roles, consistency in its experience helps form these experiences into identity. Rituals help create identity because the consistent nature of a ritual, chosen by parents and honored by the family, identifies the priorities of its members. Rituals define our family experience.

RELATIONSHIPS . . . Healthy communication between family members is critical to the development of the child's identity. Rules of engagement is that standard parents must set, communicating through conflict and pain, as well as through joy and pleasure.

The safety to be yourself and have an open and honest dialogue with the others in the family culture, creates a deep sense of relationship which allows each family member to feel a sense of belonging and a sense of self.

You guys remember the Siegel Family, don't you? Tyler and Joanne Siegel created an amazing Family Culture for their three children, Annie, Jeffrey, and Rose. This was the story of the parents' culture and Rose's truth.

Rose's siblings were both off to college which exposed the fact that Rose's voice was somewhat buried beneath the accomplishments of her siblings within the family culture Tyler and Joanne created.

You see, their family culture was built with all best intentions and great skill by these two wonderful parents. They just never thought that any one of their children would question their structure, their values, or their choices, much less not feel safe to bring it to them for discussion.

Rose could not hide her feelings anymore, once the structure had changed and she was alone with her parents. The Siegels had the courage to let Rose feel the power of her voice and the trust to make decisions that were different than her parents' preference. (Very impressive parenting!)

Family Culture is the "practice field" of life for our children. Parents supply everything that goes into the culture for our child's practice in the family experience; everything, of course, except the experience itself.

The child has their own experience of the moment and must be empowered to make decisions based on the intention of their feelings with the coaching and guidance from their parents.

RULES . . . TO LIVE BY.

Family Culture like all cultures require order for its members to learn, grow, and experience their life, peacefully. Parents create their Family Culture with their own preferences, expectations, values, morals, and ethics.

To be effective in accomplishing a safe and orderly environment for their family members to live fully in the moment, parents must establish a SET OF RULES for the Family Culture itself.

RULES are the expectations and requirements that each individual must embrace, understand, and follow for the culture to function effectively.

PARENTS ARE THE GOVERNING BODY FOR THE FAMILY CULTURE THEY CREATE.

CONSEQUENCES are the next set of circumstances the individual finds themselves facing when they choose NOT to follow the rules established by the culture.

"Success at any and all cost" as a standard for the Family Culture changes the experience of a consequence from the "next set of circumstances" we must face to "punishment" for the FAILURE that we let define us. Fear and avoidance of "punishment" forces children into the "Going Underground" behavior. Failure and mistakes cannot be seen as condemnable offenses and must be seen as part of a process of learning, growth and practice in life.

There really is nothing large or small about success or failure. They are both just moments in the process of experience.

REMEMBER . . . DELIVERY IS EVERYTHING!

Responding to those moments in the process of your child's experience rather than reacting to the consequence with judgment, will keep the moment safe and the experience whole.

FAMILY CONSTITUTION.

The Family Constitution establishes a structure of boundaries and guidelines that will allow the child to experience their own moment within the Family Culture.

Parents have an opportunity within the dynamics of this structure to coach, guide, educate their child, WHILE their child is experiencing their own decisions (whatever they may be) unobstructed by "reaction" and "judgment" of their parents. The Family Constitution must be founded in the concept of RESPECT.

RESPECT is the attitude and process of honoring someone or something through the intention to be KIND and MINDFUL of the other.

The story of the Dietrich Family shows us that the process of structure, such as the Family Constitution, is very helpful in providing order in the household and placing the responsibility for each member's behavior and attitude with the individual.

For George and Sheila Dietrich, the Family Constitution was a nice tool to remove the power struggle with their children while remaining in authority of their Family Culture.

Parenting "on the run" with no structured set of rules and consequences, makes it impossible to provide children with the safe place to have their voice and experience the intentions of their feelings, WITHOUT having to be in reaction to their parents judgment.

RITUAL, RITUALS, RITUALS . . .

Rituals help create identity. When parents designate a specific TIME and SPACE to honor the worth of an experience, it then becomes something that defines the identity of each member of the family.

We identify with our preference and we prioritize our experience around that preference. A parent's role, as I have said many times, is to create a safe place for their child to experience the intention of their feelings. RITUALS PROVIDE THAT SAFE PLACE IN THE FAMILY CULTURE.

Do you remember the story of the "ice cream cake ritual?" Something that started out as a funny misunderstanding has become a generational birthday experience that specifically identifies that family. (Goldie's meatballs for the Jewish holidays provides a similar experience for me.)

In the Dietrich Family, it was the resolve that the parents had to "ritualize" the Family Constitution that turned it from a "new exercise" that the family was attempting into a consistent PRIORITY of the Dietrich Family Culture.

FAMILY MEALS . . . The Family Meal is a perfect "safe place" for children to experience the intention of their feelings, if parents are responding and not reacting and there is a set of rules in place.

Meals are something we can count on to easily turn into ritual because, of course, we have to feed our family everyday.

The Dietrich Family Meal went from being a painful, chaotic experience to a place where within the new structure each member found their voice in a safe ritualized experience.

For the Dembo Family, our "Sunday Night Family Dinner" ritual proved to be a healing experience originally. Then as the ritual became a part of the family culture, it continued to be a part of our identity.

FAMILY MEETINGS . . . The Family Meeting is a time set aside each week for the whole family to sit down and review the upcoming schedule of activities, review the set of rules and consequences and allow each member to share thoughts, suggestions, and concerns (to have a voice in their family process).

Do you remember the Walsh Family? Steven and Rose Walsh had very high standards for the two sons, Stevey and Carson. The boys truly lived up to the standards of the Family Culture the Walsh's created for them. The parents lived in such fear that the boys would falter and used that fear as motivation to keep the boys at a high level of performance. This created a "great picture" with a "painful truth."

Stevey and Carson became so disrespectful to their parents as a reaction to their parents' lack of living in the truth of who their sons actually were.

After organizing the Family Culture, and creating rituals such as the Family Meeting, the Walsh's had weekly space to revisit the standards of the culture and gave the boys a place to represent their truth.

This ritual allowed for the respect of the truth, by empowering the boys to self-regulate (they were already) with a structured set of rules and the parents a time and place to govern.

RITUALIZED TIME WITH YOUR CHILD.

The intimacy of a reciprocal interaction between parent and child in a safe paradigm allows a child to have a voice and receive feedback. It also allows a parent to be the coach who guides and educates their child through their child's experience. **A shared ritualized time is a priceless, valuable ingredient to the safety and depth of the parent/child relationship.**

Melissa Harley's story is a wonderful example of the true need children have for individual time and experiences with their parents. The family had everything in place necessary to raise such a large number of children. Melissa however needed more and had the maturity and the voice to ask for it.

Once we were able to be creative with their complicated schedule, we created "ritualized time" for each child with each parent. These are rituals every child and parent can benefit from.

PARENTING AS A BASKETBALL METAPHOR.

A parent is the coach that teaches the skills to the player (child) necessary to self-regulate on the court of life.

In the game of basketball, there are two forms of defense that a team may use . . .

1. MAN-TO-MAN . . . The strategy is that wherever the ball handler tries to go with the ball, the defender follows step for step.
2. ZONE . . . The strategy is to let the ball handler "dribble" their ball within a certain boundary, only to intervene if they dribble beyond the approved area.

When teaching a new player (child) the rules of the game and the skills necessary to play, a coach must be willing to get onto the practice court with the player and teach using the strategies of "Man-to-Man" and "Zone."

A coach (parent) must also be willing to get off the court when the player is ready, and move to the sideline and let the player play.

The goal is to ready your child to "dribble" their ball in the largest "zone" possible . . . on the "basketball court" of their life.

"Man-to-Man" is very effective with children from birth to age 10.

"Zone" works well when the child has more developed skills to "dribble," typically from ages 10 to 18 depending on maturity and readiness.

The story of Mary Crawford and her parents teaches us as parents that our agenda just may not fit the truth of our child. If we insist on our agenda to be their truth when it clearly doesn't fit, we will be forced to keep our child in a "Man-to-Man" strategy well past when they are ready to have a "Zone" to practice the truth of their own identity.

For Mary, the more her parents forced their agenda, the more she detached herself from her own truth and went "underground" while creating an illusion for her parents.

As we have said throughout this book, the original feelings NEVER go away, and one day must again resurface.

For Mary (as for all our children,) when given a chance to figure out her own game, find space to practice her life skills, without her parents judgment BUT with their guidance, coaching and love, she found that she is an amazing "ball handler" of her own life.

Parenting is the coaching of a fluid strategy that transitions between "Man-to-Man" and "Zone" based on the skill level of the child. Without judgment and reaction, a parent can respond to the experiences of their child safely, moving on and off the court of their child's life as their child needs.

ALWAYS REMEMBER . . . As a parent, we Teach, Guide, Coach and Love our children through their OWN Experience. They're our children but its their truth.

For those of you who are parents, and for ALL OF US, who are "somebody's child," I leave you (for now) with the words from a poem written in 1996 by an award-winning poet, my daughter, Elizabeth R. Dembo:

My soul cannot be kept,
My mind cannot be held.
I am me,
I am me.
Though you want to live within me,
You cannot.
I am me,
I am me.
I go further and further away,
You run to me.
I am me,
I am me.
Give me space,

Let me be.
AND I WILL BE ME.

A "chip off the old block?" . . . Perhaps.

A child's voice speaking her own truth? . . . Absolutely!

Dr. Philip B. Dembo is Director of Life Strategies, a coaching and consulting firm specializing in relationship dynamics such as parenting. Dr. Dembo is an expert in helping parents raise amazing kids with a strong sense of self and conscience, who make good decisions, and live a life of integrity. Using simple strategies and analogies, such as basketball parenting, to help parents set boundaries, Dr. Dembo has a way of making difficult situations easy to understand and relatable for any parent. For 30 years, Dr. Dembo has helped thousands of people live better lives. His unique relationship strategies have led his clients to personal, business, sports performance and family success. His work with professional athletes, including a recent NFL kicker who was the top scorer on his team, has helped them rise to the top of their game. As an accomplished public speaker he has been featured on news programming such as Great Day St. Louis, Fox Sports Northwest, KPLR 11 News, KSDK News, and Fox 5 News San Diego. He has also served as an expert for the *St. Louis Business Journal, The Riverfront Times,* MSN Money.com, Today.com an Hollywoodlife.com. Dr. Dembo hosts his own radio talk show, THE PARENT COACH on Healthylife.net. He taught for many years at St. Louis University, adjunct, in the College of Education's Marriage and Family Therapy program. For the past 30 years he has worked in private practice, and various other settings, coaching his clients on topics related to improving the quality of their relationships and lives. In addition to parenting, Dr. Dembo has served as expert about a variety of topics including: Balancing personal and business lives, Successful partnerships, Team building, Raising children with integrity, Positive discipline, Handling change, Identity development, Confidence building, Life balance, Self-discovery, Athletic focus, Elite athletic performance.

ALSO PUBLISHED BY JACQUIE JORDAN INC.

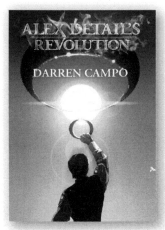

Alex Detail's Revolution
by Darren Campo

Alex Detail has been kidnapped.

Again.

Ten years ago, Alex was a child genius who saved the world from The Harvesters, a mysterious alien force that attempted to extinguish Earth's sun.

A decade later, The Harvesters have returned, but Alex is no longer a prodigy and unwilling to fight another war. So someone at The House of Nations had him drugged and placed on the last remaining ARRAY warship, which is under heavy attack. Unfortunately for Alex's mysterious kidnappers (and the world) he has lost the mega IQ that allowed him to win the last war.

Now Alex must convince the ship's food-obsessed Captain Odessa to use his risky command program to save their ship, uncover his kidnapper's devious plot, and survive the war long enough to make it to Pluto, where, underneath the planet's frozen surface lies the only force in the universe that can stop The Harvesters.

ALSO PUBLISHED BY JACQUIE JORDAN INC.

Alex Detail's Rebellion
sequel to
Alex Detail's Revolution
by Darren Campo

Alex Detail is being assassinated.

Again.

The second Harvester war has ended, but Alex has never been in greater peril. Not only is Alex being hunted by his deadly clone, the seven-year-old George Spell, he is also the target of a House of Nations plot to expose Alex's post-war experiments with The Harvesters and disgrace the genius war hero.

But when George Spell's latest attempt to assassinate Alex Detail at the New York planetarium nearly kills hundreds of people, Alex escapes death only to find his would-be assassin suddenly kidnapped by the powerful mystic, Brother Lonadoon.

Now Alex must join Captain Odessa on a covert interplanetary rescue operation where they uncover clues left thousands of years ago by an ancient race desperately trying to send a message to the future. But the message might be too late, as phenomena are revealing the beginnings of an extinction level event caused by the ongoing war between Alex Detail and George Spell, one that could lead to the destruction of the entire solar system.

ALSO PUBLISHED BY JACQUIE JORDAN INC.

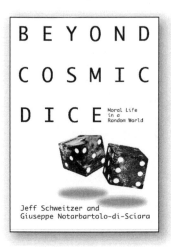

Beyond Cosmic Dice: Moral Life in a Random World

by Dr. Jeff Schweitzer and Giuseppe Nortarbartolo-di-Sciara

This is the book that ties it all together – the problems that religion creates in solving our looming problems, and the unholy environmental mess we're in. I'd say that someday we're going to have to listen to this man, but the truth is, that day is NOW.

– Bill Maher

Morality is our biological destiny. We each have within us the awesome power to create our own meaning in life, our own sense of purpose, our own destiny. With a natural ethic we are able to move beyond the random hand of birth to pave our own road to a better life. Whereas religion claims that happiness is found from submission to a higher power, a natural ethic defines happiness as the freedom to discover within ourselves our inherent good, and then to act on that better instinct, not because of any mandate from above or in obedience to the Bible, but because we can. With the ability to choose to be good comes the obligation to make that choice; choosing to be moral is what makes us special as individuals and as a species. With a natural ethic we free ourselves from the arbitrary and destructive constraints of divine interference to create a path toward a full life for which we ourselves are responsible.

ALSO PUBLISHED BY JACQUIE JORDAN INC.

The New Moral Code

Also titled
Beyond Cosmic Dice:
Moral Life in a Random World,
with a new introduction.

**by Dr. Jeff Schweitzer
and Giuseppe
Nortarbartolo-di-Sciara**

In a confusing world in which faith no longer satisfies, *The New Moral Code* paves a clear path to happiness and fulfillment. The authors provide simple and easy steps to free you from the angst of today's modern society. Learn to shed the burden of expectation created by others and pave your own road to a meaningful life of deep contentment.

ALSO PUBLISHED BY JACQUIE JORDAN INC.

NINETEEN
A Reflection of My Teenage Experience in an Extraordinary Life: What I Have Learned, and What I Have to Share

by Chelsea Krost

In *NINETEEN: A Reflection of My Teenage Experience in an Extraordinary Life: What I Have Learned, and What I Have to Share*, nineteen-year-old author, Chelsea Krost, authentically shares the simplicity and complexity of her coming of age experience. In NINETEEN, she conjures the curiosity and flavor of a personal journal left open in a teenager's room.

In NINETEEN, she conjures the curiosity and flavor of a personal journal left open in a teenager's room. In its direct approach, NINETEEN reveals the key events that teenagers face at this monumental time in their lives as experienced by Chelsea Krost. While many teens are struggling with typical angst from cat fights to cliques, many others are dealing with the downside of the advanced technological world we live in. From sexting to cyber bullying, self-esteem to depression; body image, mean girls and boy trouble,

Chelsea sheds light on the millennial mindset and its ever changing challenges and lightning speed curve balls.

Chelsea Krost is a nineteen year old radio talk show host and millennial spokesperson who has embarked on a new career as an author, sharing her inspirations, life lessons, motivation, and a voice for her peers, all through her own personal experiences and open diary.

SOON TO BE PUBLISHED BY JACQUIE JORDAN INC.

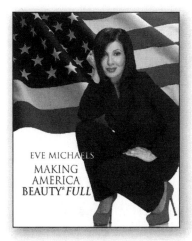

Making America Beauty Full*

by Eve Michaels

"The art and science of image is not easily accessible to Americans. If we are indeed global leaders in innovation and technology, then we have an inherent responsibility to look like global, innovative leaders."

Eve Michael, author, motivational speaker and image expert, believes that every American should know what attributes and characteristics make them unique, and how to communicate them through their visual appearance. "We have forgotten about how much our image affects our psyche and every aspect of our lives. We've let our body and grooming go unattended to, and our manners and common courtesy are becoming a thing of the past."

In America The Beauty*Full, Eve feels a personal responsibility to educate this country with an insightful and transformational journey derived from her thirty years of professional image expertise and in-depth teaching techniques on the art and science of image and beauty. Eve wants to help Americans upgrade their personal appearances to enhance their lives and careers, boost their self-esteem, and achieve the global respect they deserve. "It is my sincere dream and desire to 'Wake America Up' one person at a time, one city at a time, and one nation at this time!"

After reading this book, you will never look at image the same way again! In the courtroom of real life, Eve's compelling case for enhancing your image and taking greater pride in your appearance will win you over once and for all.

BOOKS BY JACQUIE JORDAN

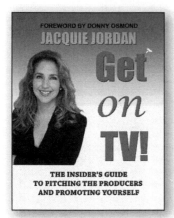

Get on TV!
The Insider's Guide to Pitching the Producers and Promoting Yourself

Expert advice on how to get booked and asked back!

"Jacquie ought to know how to get you on TV . . . she's put half the country on TV, including me."
– Maury Povich

In *Get on TV!*, Jacquie Jordan brings her expert advice straight to you – the entrepreneurs, experts, authors, and future reality stars looking to land a television spot. Jacquie shows you the ins and outs of the TV business and what you need to do to get booked (and asked back), including:

- The importance of tape and materials
- Speaking the language of the television producer
- Being persistent without being annoying
- What to do when you're booked and cancelled
- How to get asked back again and again

If you know the right moves, you can get on TV!

"Jacquie has the ability to maintain a fair balance between the voice of the project she is producing and the needs of her guests."
– John Edward, psychic medium and author of *Crossing Over*, host of John Edward: Cross Country

Jacquie Jordan has been involved in booking, supervising or producing over 10,000 television guests, as well as coaching countless people on how to get on air.

Heartfelt Marketing Allowing the Universe to be Your Business Partner

Heartfelt Marketing is for the self-inspired entrepreneur who understands their skill set; however, promotion isn't their forte.

- Learn how to get out of your own way and generate business by being of service to others.
- Release the 5 Pitfalls that spell doom for your revenue.
- Discover how the language and intention make a HUGE difference in the sale.
- Let go of the energetic tackiness in your business exchanges that screams inferiority.
- Explore the blocks that are getting in the way of business expansion.

"The skills Jacquie taught me in her book, course, and coaching have given me the keys to successfully communicate to a broad audience in a language that catches attention but never compromises the core of the meaning of my work and mission in life. This is the alchemy of heart-based marketing; turning your invisible passionate emotions about your work, topic, or product, and turning it into a sound-track that will grab attention and invite a wide audience into your mission."
– Christine Stevens, UpBeat Drum Circles

"Jacquie Jordan sends a heartfelt message that we can be strong in business and still come from the Heart. This book represents where business is going – from being a one-track money model to an expression of who we are and one that can help humanity as well."
– Ali Brown, Ali International LLC, millionaire entrepreneur coach